GO SEO YOURSELF

Get Motivated, Break-Through And Find A #Job Using The Internet!

BY

Dan Gudema

ISBN: 1976118417
ISBN-13: 978-1976118418

DEDICATION

I am dedicating this book to my wife Linda Delucca,
who believes in me when no one else will.

CONTENTS

ACKNOWLEDGMENTS

I want to use this opportunity to acknowledge everyone who influenced me and helped me or influenced me while putting this book together. People like Jonathan Gudema, Craig Henderson, Heath Jones, John Kemp, Bob Norville, Aramas Kaloustian, Brandon Esposito, Brad Feld, Ben Chodor, Mark Ernst, Hal Robinson, Ed Donofrio, Mark Griggs, Tom Delucca, Lane Vance, Stacy Hallman, Francis Fytton, JT Bruce, Vince Gelormine, Michael Clarke, Darren Wadholtz RIP, Terry Aaronson, Marc Wigder, Michelle Gudema, Mark Brooks, Marc Lesnak, Leanne Webb, Dan Verkman, Dennis Wakabayashi, Mike O'Donnell, Mike Lingle, Dr. Kenneth Huang, Mark Brown, Amanda Zook, Tristan Daley, Offain Gunasekara, Brandi Chaney, James Nolan, Franc Nemanic, Peter Shankman, Dr. Derrick Huang, George Dubec, Berny Dohrman, Adam Kravitz, Lance Gilbert, Abhi Puttanna, Martin Amtman, Valerie Jones, Brett Mullins, Deborah Johnson, Karen Herman Bruce Cohen, Young Kim, Alex Funkhouser, Andy Klepner.

1

THE JOB APOCALYPSE

Are you out of work right now?

I had been in and out of a couple tech startups, my own consulting business, and my own failed web agency right before my job apocalypse.

All of those short-term careers had failed. And we needed a job to pay the bills. I had a family to support and I was burning through my 401k plan month after month.

Have you hit a point in your career where you're at a mid-life career crisis?

For the first time in my 27 year career, I did not have a clue what to do about finding a job!

Let's just say I was often both under-qualified and overqualified for the same job position if that is possible.

Does This Apply To You?

My broad skill-set was not what contemporary companies desired. I blame a lot of that on being involved with startups. I had a broad set of skills. I was not an expert at anything in particular, except how to start-up a tech business. That's not exactly what corporations want from most employees!

Large corporate employers using head-hunters want specific narrowly scoped skills. Head-hunters want a specific type of skill they know will have a chance of winning that job. That's how they get paid. They want a person who knows x, not a-z. In fact, they want a person to not mention anything else they know. They want a chicken and not a turkey, and though you may be both, that has to be hidden for now.

I did not have a specialty at that point when I needed one that I could hang my hat on, which they could easily point to that was relevant in the marketplace.

Is this your current situation?

Do you have what amounts to a limited range of your job prospects?

I had years of real-world experience, a vast amount of online Marketing, IT, Web, Software Development,

Management, Finance, and Analytics experience. I was a jack of all trades.

And as you can see I was also a writer. But being above average at a lot of things will only get you a token to ride on the subway when you just need a job to pay the bills.

I knew too much and I knew too little.

When larger corporations hire new employees, the employees fall into two categories, skilled workers or management. I was at the management level, yet, I had not been a serious manager/director in at least 5 years.

Trust me I was a manager and director of several large Fortune 500 companies. But it was not recent and most job titles and areas of expertise had changed a lot in that short time period. What is hot right now, 3 years from today will be out of favor.

I had been a Web Manager, now a position that was a relic of the past. Yet somehow web teams were being managed out there!

It is hard to believe Web Manager has disappeared as a common management position today. In fact, management positions are less and less part of corporate America. So, when it came to a management position I was not a great candidate in the eyes of the headhunter. Almost all management is hired directly from an existing management position. Overall corporate America today is relatively flat with 90% of employees being skill-based. That is why you need to always have a skill in your back pocket!

I was running low on cash and I had a wife who was a stay-at-home mother. So I needed to work. I needed benefits. I have a mortgage to pay. I have 2 kids in elementary school, one who had some special needs that I was paying for special eye therapy at the time. These things all add up to a lifetime of savings disappearing quickly.

I blamed the market and employers. I blamed everything and everybody. Eventually, I would have to stop blaming people and companies and take whatever job I could get. I would have been a Starbucks Tasterista if I had to go into Consulting, let's just get that out of the way.

I had been a startup consultant for several years, jumping between projects. Just happens most of the startups and projects ended when the founder's funds ran dry and often my shares became worthless. I had attempted my own startup, an events company that invited startups to pitch. That startup was not a money maker, though I had thoroughly enjoyed doing it. But there is a difference between new businesses that make a profit and a business that is a write-off. I had gambled and lost. It happens to all of us at some point in time.

I even tried to build out my own web agency with my

wife, but what I found in trying to compete using Thumbtack and other lead generation systems is what I call "The Race To The Bottom". The "Race To The Bottom" is my referral to competing with overseas workers and companies that hire 20-25-year-old workers that rely on low wage workers to do the work. The whole concept of the modern web agency is now based on being able to outsource everything to lower cost workers. That was something we were not prepared to do.

I had been a software developer and I had managed a large e-commerce team at a hosting company. I had worked on an e-commerce catalog business that grew from $0 to $500 million in online sales. I had been a project manager and founder for at least 4 startups and was an expert in web analytics and digital marketing. I had even co-founded a startup that grew to over 100 cities and had become the largest speed dating company in the US called Pre-Dating.com and was sold to Cupid in 2005.

But none of that mattered now because, at the point when I needed to find a job for real, my skill-set was out of whack with the marketplace. The job market is a rapidly changing environment and a merry-go-round. Once you get off that merry-go-round and want to get back on, it is difficult to jump on and find your feet.

So, what is this book about really about?

It's pretty clear from the title.   Around the time I attempted to rehabilitate my career so I could get a job and work full-time, I began a process that would eventually transform my career and how others perceive me. I was able to completely turn the job search methods I had used to find work in the past inside out, upside down and driven in reverse.

The techniques I used to find work came naturally to me because I love to write and communicate and I was already active on social media and a regular blogger. Using the Internet effectively makes sense to me. What I did not understand back when I started this process, is this method I was using was much more than a glitch I had discovered in the search for a job.

It was the NEW WAY of finding a job!

It would become what I believe is the new world order of looking for work. It was the switch from push to pull. Instead of searching for work, the jobs began to find me.

Some of the techniques I used had an immediate impact. Within several months I was starting to feel the change as I gave up applying and started to feel the pull. Instead of applying aimlessly, I started to receive call after call. Almost 2 years later, when I was in between jobs and back on the market, I was able to turn up my techniques again and immediately I am getting found and called and emailed. From the very beginning, I went from being the job hunter to being the hunted.

I had successfully reversed the job matching process and eventually, I landed a job which made total sense for me.

This process had little to do with applying or searching for work or even the normal process of networking. It was not from the hard work of a job search. It was the entrepreneurial method of doing less with more. I used the Internet and my personal community to get so well indexed by Google and every possible method of getting found online, that eventually, this reversed my fortunes.

But how did I change that process around without going back to school or having a major win in my career on my resume?

In the past 2 years, I have literally received as many as 10 to 20 job solicitations a day by email and phone calls. In the first year, I ended up having to use a spreadsheet to track and remember all the information about the many Fortune 500 companies which contacted me.

At the peak of my job search, I was flown into cities around the country by Fortune 500 companies competing for my attention. Eventually, I need to track carefully every employer and headhunter that I was working with and write down the contact info into an excel spreadsheet to track my progress. Often I would mix up the names of agents calling me, so I had to make sure they were tracked properly. I also had to make sure I was not going down the same path with a particular employer over and over to reduce the chances of confusion and duplication which can quickly end a job application. If you are submitted to a job more than once at many corporations it can be a problem.

In the end, I was contacted by over 40 Fortune 500 companies over the first 6 months of my job search. I have had my email box overfilled, been texted and had headhunters over-fill my voicemail many, many, many times. Here is a real copy of the spreadsheet I had to use to keep up with the names of the companies that contacted me.

	A	B	C	D	E	F
	D30			f_x		
1	Job Application Tracking				Talked	
2					Around	Remote
3		Company	Location	Title	Date	Allowed
4	1	PNC Bank	Pittsburgh	Senior Web Analyst	Oct 20?	Yes
5	2	Cisco	Raleigh	Senior Web Developer	3-Nov	Yes
6	3	Staples	Framingham	Senior Web Analyst		No
7	4	Office Depot	Boca Raton	Email Analyst		No
8	5	AT&T	Atlanta	Web Anaytics Architect		No
9	6	Verizon	Warren, N. Virg.	Web Analytics Consultant	20-Oct	No
10	7	Tmobile	Bothell	Web Analytics Consultant	15-Oct	No
11	8	Verizon	Piscataway	Senior Analyst/Manager	25-Oct	No
12	9	Echostar	Englewood	Adobe Analytics		No
13	10	Verizon Wireless	Irving Texas	Web Designer/Web Dev.		No
14	11	Alaskan Air	Tukwila, WA	Ecommerce Analyst	2-Nov	No
15	12	?	DC	Ecommerce Analyst		?
16	13	Walmart Labs	Sunnyvale	Web Analytics Consultant	15-Oct	No
17	14	CBS Sportsline	Fort Lauderdale	Data Engineer	1-Oct	
18	15	AutoNation	Fort Lauderdale	Web Analyst	3-Nov	
19	16	Adobe Systems (TCS)	San Jose	Web Analytic Consultant	5-Nov	
20	17	Home Depot	Atlanta	Web Analytic Manager	10-Nov	No
21	18	?	Orlando	Senior Web Analyst	10-Nov	
22	19	Stanley Black & Decker	Baltimore	Web Analytic Manager - Digital Marketing	Nov 2-Nov 12	No
23	20	CSAA (AAA)	Phoenix	Senior Web Analytics Data Analyst	14-Nov	Yes
24	21	TIAA	Charlotte	Senior Web Analyst	18-Nov	

For the last 2 jobs and consulting gigs I worked, I was directly contacted by the employer or the owner of the company themselves. Being contacted directly by employers is ultimately what you want to do.

I quickly got to the point where I no longer applied for jobs. If you do your homework and work hard at planning out your online universe, there will be no need to waste time applying for anything.

Employers will find you directly!

But How Do Employers Find Me?

The answer is quite clear. You need to rebuild yourself online to be found correctly.

You need to get so well discovered as an authority in your field online that you show up first when they are searching for a candidate.

But knowing where employers and head-hunters search is critical. There are a good 25 places they may find you I will mention in this book. In fact, there are so many places, resume sites, LinkedIn, social networks, blog sites, event sites, book sites, and your own website, it is actually an infinite sum game. You can be in as many cloud-based services online you want to be listed in. It is all up to you. It is all up to how much work you want to put into the project of furthering your career. It is also about making smart decisions about where and how you show up. That is why you will be buying and reading this book!

This is what I refer to as SEO'ing yourself. The name of

this book is ***GO SEO YOURSELF*** for a reason. SEO stands for "Search Engine Optimization". The way SEO works are words, information, images, and video gets run through an algorithm that determines the final order of contents on Google, Bing, and Yahoo when you search. The same is true of resume sites, LinkedIn and every website that has content on it. Yes, even within every resume site there is SEO. Google's Search Engine today has become a lot more sophisticated using changing algorithms, Artificial Intelligence (AI) and produce what we call authority. Authority gets you found higher in search results. That's all you need to know for now. The farther you read into this book, the more you will learn and know about SEO and the better you will get at it.

Getting properly SEO'd personally and building personal authority to get discovered is what I recommend you do for yourself to find have the same results I achieved. This book is a guide to that process.

There is much more to learning SEO than it appears. SEO is not just about getting found higher up in the search engines. Getting higher up is important, but what is more important are not the results of your SEO work, but the journey. If you follow my personal SEO process you will not just get found better, you will be more informed, better connected and you will find it impacts your career overall. So, this is not just a gimmicky book about being higher in Google page rank. Go SEO Yourself is about personal transformation and using technology effectively for your own personal achievement. It impacts your future and it could impact your spouse, your family, and your retirement. This book is about the real process of using the Internet effectively!

This process is the new world order in finding work! By finding work I am referring to both a job and consulting work. You can work directly with an employer or have your own company. It does not matter which direction you go in. There are employers out there that need to find you if you were findable! This is the process you need to put in place for your future!

You need to rethink your process of looking for work and start this method as soon as physically possible. I say physically possible because when I am working full-time I still do these methods and it takes physical fortitude to pop out a blog entry late Friday night before I go to bed, make sure my kids have done their homework or sit here and write this book. This small amount of work you be doing every day has an impact on your life!

The work you put into getting yourself established online will be worth it in the end. Even if you are already successful and know how to easily find a job, you still want to find a job that is always a better fit, pays more, and is closer to home. If you are starting up an agency or consulting firm, you still need to go through all the same processes we discuss in this book. We all want a better job with better benefits, that we like better, with bosses we would rather work for that that allows you to work from home or other things which are important in your life!

But and reading this book is much more than about getting found by employers for jobs. It's about being a thought leader online. It's about creating your online persona that is bigger, better and larger than the next guy. It's about the next job and the job after that. It's about your future and the future technology world we have entered. It is only just beginning, and if you do not want to get left behind this is the place to start and get yourself in order. Your competition is already online big time doing a lot of the activities I will mention in this book. This process is about creating the right mix about you of content, positioning, building personal authority, and using various social media in order to be found properly.

There are so many factors involved getting found online and so many activities you should be taking.

One thing is clear. If you want to find a job, switch careers, move up the corporate ladder or create a new business or become an online guru, you need to create an online persona that is so superior to others, you are the person that employers, customers, and networking contacts absolutely need to connect with and hire.

You need to become the Go-To Guy or Gal! Even within your corporation, men and women that are the right social networking giants are the next leaders.

But you need to get yourself SEO'd right!

I say right because you can get it all wrong. The traditional boundaries and hierarchies you may be used to in your career and from previous job searches in corporate America are breaking down because of online communities, social media and a new world order are about to rise up. Sadly most corporate employees just do their job and are satisfied with where they are at in life and don't build out a social media following. Most are computer savvy but just don't know how to navigate the online world. And many are fearful of building up a large social media following because it may take away from their employer and employment. I get that, and I cover that in this book. You may have to find a balance while you are working full-time and understand the boundaries!

Quite honestly, if your employer leaves you and you are laid off, you will need a large network to work with to find a job. The average career today at one employer is 4.4 years. If you have not yet started building your community 2 years ago and building your LinkedIn profile out 2 years ago… you will have to start this today. And guess what? In a short period of time, you too can be at par or ahead of most of your competition for work. You have to start building out your community today. You will become an expert within a month and ultimately an Internet guru! Get started now, and keep reading onward in this book! Buy it today and read it and take actions, if you have not already done so.

This book will cover everything you should and must be doing online to build yourself up, to not just be found, but be followed, be a leader and ultimately get you to the next level. It will cover the transformation you personally need to go through. And it's not all SEO techie stuff. A lot of this is your attitude and experiencing new things like being a leader and creating groups and giving the directions and not just following.

What's funny about leadership is I have known 100 CEOs, VPs, Directors and other corporate leaders I have worked for and consulted with who don't really have a leadership bone in their bodies. In fact, they often are quick to shy away from being the person who starts something than anybody else. Most are good at doing the work, not creating or leading. The next time you are at a company with a layoff, notice which executives stay around the day of the big layoff. Most top executives traditionally avoid conflict. Corporate executives are often great at implementing for the corporation. There has to be a reason they are in charge. Trust me it is often not brains, but their brawn and ability to carry out the orders from the top. The current corporate leaders we typically know today are not the type of person who will be a future leader. Future leaders know how to start and lead, not just follow. This online world gives us a chance to be the fair-haired kid and get ourselves ahead if we take action and do what we need to, to be successful.

Carrying out the techniques in this book worked for me. I was able to turn my career around. I put in quite a bit of time and energy in order to figure out what are the best methods to get SEO'd personally.

And this is not just about LinkedIn. LinkedIn is just one online platform you need to master. There are now up to 25 places online I will recommend you pursue, join and master, develop authority, build SEO and create your own personal community.

But the specific places online are not what's important. You can put your pen down now. You still need to read this book to understand how everything works. It is not just about a resume anymore! What is important is your message and how you are perceived by the marketplace.

It is also important for you to follow a rigidly well thought out and consistent implementation method. You need to repeat, repeat, repeat and consistently be consistent. That will change how you are viewed. You need to determine your personal strategy, especially one with a regular cadence you can handle. Think about yourself. How often do you log in to LinkedIn and post? How often or have you ever written a blog article? Do you know why people are even writing blog articles? How often do you update your resumes on the top 6 job sites?

This book will cover blogging, tweeting, publishing eBooks, websites, Meetup, SEO in general, Facebook and a ton of internet recommendations.

I will let you in on my personal secrets that will be obvious to you once you learn how to do it yourself!

But as I have said from the beginning of this book, it is not the tricks of the Internet that will land you where you need to go in your career, it is your strategy and how that strategy is perceived by your peers.

This book will cover SEO (Search Engine Optimization), but mainly from the personal perspective. If you don't know about SEO, it is time you get acquainted.

SEO used to only be in the realm of online marketing consultants. SEO is how well you show up in Google searches. It's about getting discovered through Google and other search engines by showing up higher based on the keywords people search for.

There are a dozen great primary SEO website platforms that we will cover.

Primary SEO platforms are online places that Google searches better than anywhere else. You can use them as a way to get listed higher on Google. Did you know that?

Primary SEO platforms are websites that get indexed by Google exceptionally well because they are the best of the best and they create tons of rich content that Google consumes every day. That is why Google gives them authority! Good examples are Amazon, eBay, and Craigslist. Hmm... You must be wondering. What do these sites have to do with you personally? Honestly, any site which gets top billing at Google is a place you should investigate. To get your own products on your own website listed on Google for instance in a tough overly sought after online market is virtually impossible to do right away today. That's because every company in that industry has paid for SEO services and Google is saturated with too many websites to index on the subject. Yet, a listing on Amazon goes right to the top of Google. That means if you get nicely on Amazon, you have a better chance of getting higher up on Google through Amazon!

There are positives and negatives to SEO. This book will cover the good, the bad and the ugly.

You want companies looking for great new talent to find you. You want them to be compelled to get in contact with you. To be found, you must become a thought leader online.

Is This How You Will Find Your Next Job?

If you are in the middle of a job search, the first thing you need to do is get rid of the concept of a "Job Search". Searching for a job the old fashion way of sending out resumes and knocking on doors today can be a waste of your time and energy.

That's because of a little unknown principle I learned back in college studying political science. We used to call it the problems of democracy. While there are a ton of great things about democracies, there are also some negatives. Remember, the US is not a full democracy; it is what we call a republic. In a republic, we elect people who make decisions for us. The people don't vote on bills, representatives do.

With the growth of the Internet, there is one aspect of a democracy that can be problematic. That specific problem has to do with the availability of information.

Years ago when I first looked for work when I graduated from the University of Maryland, we would get the local paper and read the help wanted ads. Growing up in North Jersey, The New Jersey Star-Ledger had as many as 100 pages of job ads every Sunday. This was right before the internet grew and changed the world of information today. It was long before the great outsourcing of work, where tons of jobs were sent overseas.

Clearly, local jobs around the country were only known to locals back then who applied to those jobs. If you wanted a job in another city like New York City, you needed to buy a New York City paper like The New York Times to learn about an opening. Back then most people did not have the energy to look at job listings if they were working full-time.

The Internet changed everything with automated search tools. Now, not only do local, full-time working employees automatically know about new job openings, but the entire world is aware of all job openings within an industry. So a guy in South Florida can apply for a job in Seattle. A person in New York City can apply quickly for a job in Timbuktu. Even more so, everybody who is working now automatically knows of every open position on the globe at any moment.

What this means is there is a massive multiplier of job applicants.

Years ago a local job opening could get 5, 10 at most 20 applicants. Today because of the openness and speed of the Internet, jobs can get hundreds or thousands of applicants.

More specifically, employers are being forced to rely heavily on head-hunters today to weed out 99% of the applicants. Head-hunters can easily find the top 1% of candidates by finding the best resumes. The problem with this is often these top candidates are working. Meanwhile, working job candidates are leveraged, where they can take or leave a job that is open. Working job candidates can pick and choose what jobs they desire to apply for. They don't mind being picked 1st for a job they are not interested in. If you are not employed right now, what they have done is moved you down the ladder in the potential for being selected for an interview and made it difficult for you to get noticed.

So, the end result for unemployed work candidates who have been out of the job market for any length of time is they will struggle to break back into the job market because the best candidates are the ones who are working in the eyes of the employers. That is the logic among employers and it seems to make logical sense if you think it through. It is a dog eat dog world out there, where everyone working has a strategic advance over the unemployed.

Are you at a point in your career where you have hit the ceiling and cannot break through or change to a career path that makes financial sense?

You Need To Stop Now And Change What You Are Doing!

Have you taken a short break from your corporate career to work on a startup, spent time taking care of your kids, a parent or another family member or just needed a break and are now going back to work?

Good Luck getting back to work right away. I have been there and it sucks.

Why are you reading Go SEO Yourself?

Are you just a bit curious about that title?

Why did I write this book?

It was necessary to tell my story and help others.

How I Got Started On This Book?

The foundation of this book started with a LinkedIn Article I wrote in 2016 called "How To Find A Job When You Are In The 5 Ohs?"

I wrote the article just being honest and upfront with my friends and business associates about the strategies, problems, and issues I was facing in going from a startup person back to being a management corporate person at age 50 and what I was experiencing. It's an experience almost everybody goes through.

It was around the summertime when I wrote that online article. I received several thousand views and got tons of follows.   Six months earlier I had undertaken an experiment in personal SEO, *Search Engine Optimization* for the purpose of finding a job.

I am assuming everybody knows what SEO means by now. If you work in marketing, technology and you keep up with all things digital you will know that SEO means getting found higher in Google Searches.

But SEO means so much more to web marketers. It really has come to stand for what we call "natural" search. Natural search means we get found "naturally" without cost unlike through paid ads on Google we call Pay Per Click and a dozen other paid services.

The List

I have put together a list at the end of this book of what I believe are online websites and services you need to quickly get up to speed on and conquer as soon as you can. All of this may seem overwhelming. These websites may all seem like they are not connected or make no sense, but they are connected. You may not have the right experience to do some of the online activities I recommend in this book. Well, change that! And start doing it! These online activities are in this book for a reason, and I would take them all very seriously.

If you want to succeed, you need to master these parts of the web that others you admire have already succeeded in. And you need to take my advice to heart. A lot of the advice I give you in this book are right from my own personal community. Remember, one of the things you need to master is your own community. I learned so much from my mentors and personal community and I nurtured that community in so many ways, that just that part of career management is crazy important!

As you master each of these specific areas you will find your career changing. You may even find you don't need a real job because what you have learned is so valuable in the marketplace you can now be a full-time consultant or even an online SEO marketing consultant! I highly recommend you develop and master these websites and concepts. The following chapters will cover each area I feel is important and how I handled them and what to do in specific cases to professionalize or master certain cloud-based services.

Once again, get over your fear and put in the time to be a leader and do these things properly or at least at a level that appears professional. It will transform you and your career. We are going to cover a ton of tips and specific points that will make sense.

Through these chapters, we will cover all the ways that I was able to get myself found, discovered and followed. But more importantly, they built up what I refer to as an online persona that was more a whole puzzle than the pieces. Together it painted a picture of YOU as no resume or LinkedIn profile could ever show YOU.

Doing all this online persona and community creation was not just about SEO when I started. That was not the point for me. For me, it was truly about the message and communication points I personally present to the world. But the two are so intertwined, it is worth noting that you will transcend who you were in your career if you go through this process. You will come out of the other side a different person!

Should You Still Pursue Traditional Job Search Methods?

The traditional method of calling a headhunter when you are out of work today makes very little sense. The odds that the one you contact will be able to hook you up with a gig they control the business relationship that is right for you is like 1 out of 100. In fact, I recommend you stop applying and searching and start working you're your personal online profiles and online reputation. You can work 100x harder in searching for a job than working one time in setting up yourself online and receiving requests. Searching for and contacting headhunters is a waste of time and energy. Let head-hunters and employers contact you while you spend your time preparing your personal SEO!

Spending time with job shoppers and headhunters who want to be your exclusive rep will waste your time. You need to deal with them, trust me, but it has to be on your time frame, at your leisure, not theirs. When you have an offshore headhunter leave you what I call a time bomb in your voicemail, don't rush to get back to them. Everyone has a sense of urgency, but you need to control the sense of urgency. If they really want to get in touch with you, they can wait. The speed of getting back to this person never got me a job offer any faster.

A head-hunter time bomb is when a head-hunter leaves you a voicemail that says you have 5 minutes to call back because the employer needs a response immediately. You have to value your time, not the head-hunters! There will be other opportunities.

Most of us use a head-hunter to apply for jobs because we feel it has to be done because it is a low hanging fruit and you never know…

One time it did work for me, but about 100 times it did not. You should not continue to do the same thing over and over with a 1% chance it will work. What head-hunters are really doing with you is trying to fit a square peg into a round hole. And every once in a while a smaller square fits in a round hole. That's why we often end up on job interviews for jobs we are not qualified for or not exactly the best fit. We go for it, but it is a waste of time, almost every time.

In fact, meeting with headhunters and going over their listings may actually psychologically limit you so much that you may actually start believing there is not a job for you out there, and it can make you really think you can't find a job. That is what has happened to me when I had headhunters "Looking" for me.

I have been friends with guys who own job agencies for over 20 years in South Florida. They will be the first to tell you we'll call you, don't call us. Time is money, so if you are going to go down this road and waste your time, that is your decision.

Think of meeting with head hunters as networking and not job searching, because it is often a big waste. But as you know this old standby method has to be investigated at least to the point where it is not costing you more than it is worth. They say for instance that if you already have been an executive in a specialized industry, then an executive headhunter makes sense. What does not make sense is ignoring the 25 other ways to get discovered online and just rely on this one way to get found, because you are really limiting your possibilities.

2

<u>GET ON THE TOP TEN JOB SITES!</u>

If you are looking for a job, you need to be on every job site that employers search. That means that being on just one site like DICE or Linkedin is not enough. You need to upload your resume to the top ten job sites because that is the place that head-hunters search. It is not a mystery If you do the work and put your profile on every one of these sites, you will find a job! But, it is also very important to not waste too much time looking for jobs on these websites.

Placing your resume on these top websites is probably for most of you reading the most important place to start your job search, even more than LinkedIn and other websites types we will mention in this book.

This book covers an extensive amount of search engine rich places you need to put yourself online. It also covers methods I have used in changing how the market views you personally. Job sites are the low hanging fruit. That means it needs to be done and has to be done even before LinkedIn. It will be the first place many headhunters will turn.

The question is, do you want to be found by a headhunter or an employer directly?

Quite honestly, you really want to bypass the headhunters. Being on all the top job sites can accomplish both tasks. To get to the employer you need to be out there and available and easily found through both a Google search, on LinkedIn and on job resume site searches.

When I first started looking for work online I found the way job sites work had reversed from 15 years ago. Years ago you would apply for each job individually. That may seem to be an easy enough thing to do today, but obviously, you are competing with so many applicants, that it is sometimes better to look at the not-so-obvious methods.

One of those not so obvious methods is to upload your resume to all the job sites nicely SEO'd. Seems like a simple thing to know. Well, it was not so obvious to me for some reason at first. For many people looking for a job, the obvious is not so obvious. A lot of this is counter-intuitive. That's because many of us, especially if we are over 40, have developed patterns of how we think the world works. While the way you have always looked for a job may still be tried and proven method for you personally, there is always what we don't know.

You may still be thinking you need to search and apply for jobs. I personally believe applying is a waste of your time and energy. If you do things right, the jobs will find you! Go ahead and apply, but don't forget to do the things I mention here.

It took me several years to realize the best way to be found was to be everywhere you can technically appear. All Job sites have an upload resume and build a profile feature today.

If you look carefully all 10 of the sites we will mention in this section all have a place to upload your resume and create a profile. Each one has a relatively easy to use way to get your resume onto them. And once again we need to stop using the old terms and get onto the new terms. Resume really refers to a piece of paper. The new word is tags. Tags are the words, keywords or search terms that get your profile, blog or social media tweet or entry discovered! So your job is to not just get your resume on these 10 job sites, they need to be well tagged with the search terms to get yourself found!

Also, you need to fill out all the form fields these job sites collect. They may seem superfluous or unimportant, like a picture of you. Your picture is important! Get a great picture ready and upload it to all these job sites.

You should try to create a picture that shows you in your

best and truest form, preferably positive, yet professional. Mine shows me smiling and my head is cocked at a slight angle to show people that I am a little bit fun, real and have something to say.

Resume photos may be the difference in getting contacted about a job. So make the most of it. Do not upload skulls or happy faces. The intent is to show who you are. Don't put up an emoji!

Part of being well SEO'd is creating enough media and keyword content that get fed into the job search engines as possible. Media refers to images and video and sometimes audio. I will also refer to each of these job search sites as separate job search enginess

There are other types of text content you can add in these resume listings, beyond a photo or your picture, You need to optimize your listing. This means include information and awards and any field they offer to let you fill in. Do not leave any fields unfilled. Maximize this area of your profile in order to get found. Those extra fields are the search engine tagging that will get you found and multiply your ability to get listed higher on job sites and higher on Google. This is SEO! You need to take advantage of what SEO pros call "SEO juice" to maximize getting found. Don't waste it.

Another factor about these job sites to consider is the longevity of the job sites. I have been called by an employer or headhunter about a job where they are reading off lines from my resume which is over 10 years old. That means that these job sites are here to stay and information we put on them needs to be updated on a regular basis or they get stale. They will be around in 10 years and possibly 20 years or longer. Will you still be working? Hell yeah. We will all try to work as long as we can. At least some of us will continue working well into our retirement. We need to make sure our personal brand and representation and how people view us is maintained just like a business or your employer. You need to protect this brand and update of all these job sites That is your way of controlling how you are viewed and perceived. Let them get out of date, and you are who you once were. We used to put our resume away and move on to the real job every time we were hired. In today's fast moving society with the Internet, we need to do periodic upkeep on our brand on a regular basis just in case we have to start our careers over again.

By the end of this book and this process, you will be a new person. You may actually have a whole new job and career or be a consultant or have an amazing startup. Either way you need to make sure you are keeping it all relevant and up to date.

Eliminate The Job-A-Nator.

One of the things that everybody applying for jobs has experienced is the horrors of the job-a-nator as I call it. The job-a- nator is an AI engine that runs when you upload your resume. It tries to convert your resume into tags and shove your jobs, experiences, and schooling into database fields or online buckets. It is often so bad, you end up having to spend a good hour redoing your perfect resume in this horrible system. Luckily some of the job sites have eliminated the job-a- nator. Some have finally allowed you to upload a Word doc or PDF, where you just pop a print resume up there. Then there are job sites that will offer to pull your job history from either LinkedIn or Facebook. If you have your LinkedIn in order, that is great. Don't bother using Facebook for your history. You can, but once again you will have to go back in and add your entire resume over again. In fact, I now run away from job sites that have the job-a- nator…

SEO once again is critical to this process. Don't be afraid to have all your information searchable on those job sites. Also, just because your resume is on a job site does not mean the world can see it. The resumes are specifically not searchable by Google Search but by headhunter searches. And they have their own type of SEO within the job search site itself.

The sophistication of categorization and tagging within each job site depends on the quality of search jost sites provide to headhunters. You need to make sure your online resume has every possible search term within it. Being diligent at search engine optimization of your keywords within these resumes makes it possible for the internal search engine to find you. In fact, it will get you found and contacted over and over and over. That is why you should not stop at exactly the wording you know, but rather the words that "headhunters" and their minions are searching for. The search terms you use today may be great, but you have to put in what the employers are searching for and want and need to find. I was an expert at Google Analytics and I had worked with Omniture Analytics. Omniture Analytics had been acquired by Adobe, so I added the words "Adobe" and "Marketing Cloud" to all my resumes and profiles. That allowed employers and headhunters to easily find me. Don't make it hard for the headhunters. Make it easy.

As you know, the world changes and life changes. In 2001, the big job site you would focus all your energy on would have been Monster. Things have changed in how the job search engines worked 15 years ago, 10 years ago, 5 years and now in the past 2 years to 6 months it is changing once again. You need to keep up with the changes and use what is best for you to optimize the way the system works. So, if your goal is to get found for a job, instead of wasting your time applying, then your job is to get listed well by uploading your resume and creating full profiles on the top ten job sites in this order below, with notes.

In my search online for the top ten job sites I ended up settling on the following list of job sites. The very top of this list was Indeed.com at the time. I am going to give you some of my opinions on these websites and how they have worked for me or not worked for me.

Indeed.com

Reason To Place Resume On Indeed: Indeed has built up the best SEO on Google of any job site for natural search listings, which means they get big-time traffic, have done the work for good categorization and Indeed resumes are indexed by Google as well.

Indeed, if you have not already figured this out is the job site of job sites. They are an aggregator of job listings. What makes Indeed so special is they are the best at SEO of all the other job sites. That means, of course, they come up first on Google for almost all job listings. They do this through relevant job site content like by category, job title, industry and other SEO techniques. They always have fresh and new content which makes Google love them and a little thing I will mention a few times in this book called Rich Snippets and Rich Cards. All of that means they get found the best on Google.

And being the job site of all job sites makes Indeed the

number one place to put your resume. Not sure if everybody looking for work has noticed this, but they have a place to log in and upload your resume. You need to start on Indeed right there if you have not already started.

Initially, Indeed only focused on job listing consolidation from other job sites. Because of their amazingly well-done SEO, they have moved to the top of the heap when both job seekers and job shoppers are looking for positions.

Notice if you search for a job like "web analytic expert" on Google, Indeed will come up in the search results. Why? Because they have followed the SEO conventions of getting found on Google so well, they are right at the top. And trust me, Indeed was late to this SEO game. But all of that does not matter now. For now Indeed is the top place to get found.

Riding the coat-tails of Indeed you can break through and have your information found close to the top of the SEO pyramid. Indeed.com allows you to post your resume there and then that info is shared with Google. Indeed is a must for you to fill out, first!

And until another group knocks them from the top of the Google searches they are the top SEO resume website.

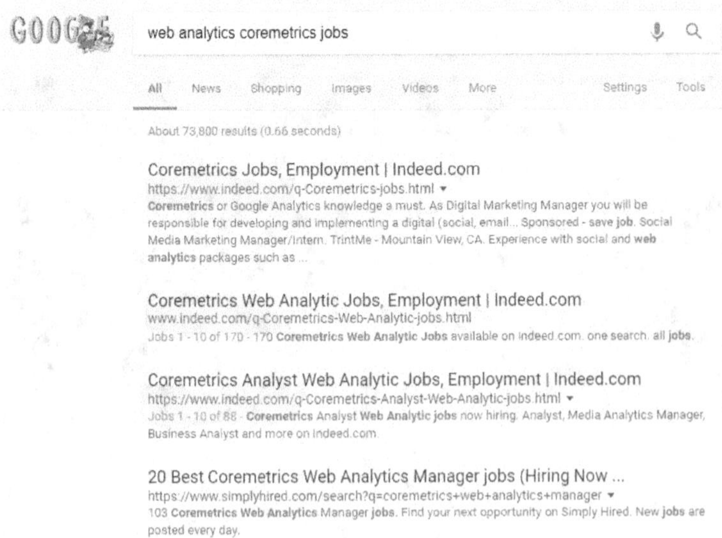

Notice in this Google search for Coremetrics jobs how Indeed shows up as the first 3 results in the search results.

LinkedIn

Reason To Build Profile On Linked: LinkedIn is the king of job profile sites. This is less about SEO and more about your brand image. Plus this is where employers who want to bypass head-hunters search the most.

LinkedIn is an obvious answer where you need to be listed and profiled and almost everybody knows this. Yet, I would have to measure almost all the other websites as just as good for places to get found. So they are great for networking and being found by employers, but they have limited how much content is searchable by

Google.

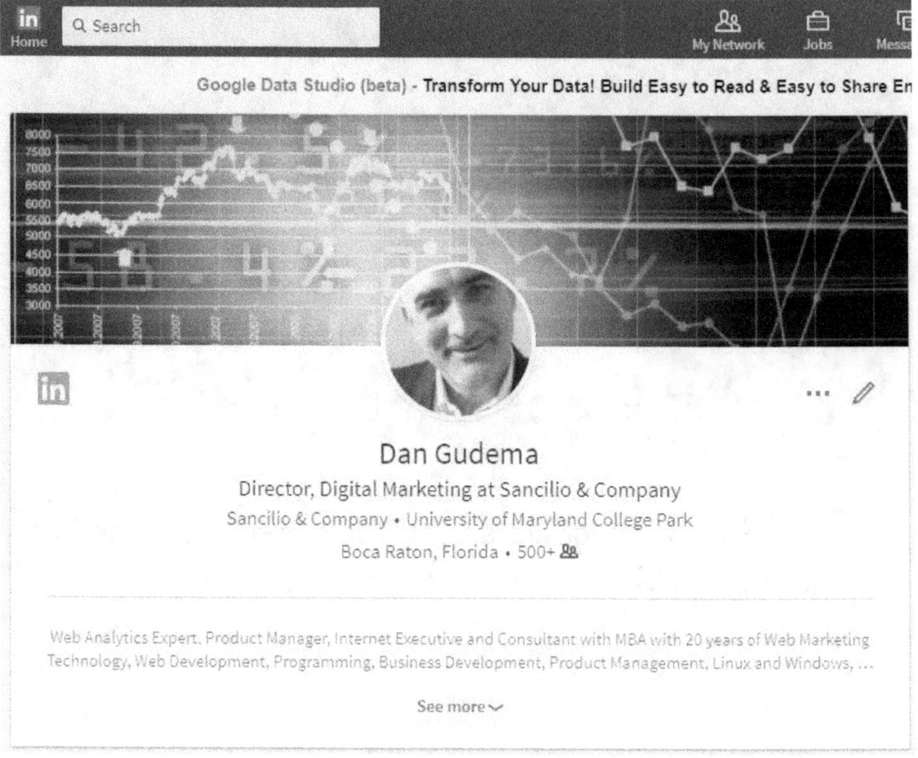

LinkedIn makes it possible for direct employers to research and learn about you. That research and learning is much, much more than a resume. Using every inch of LinkedIn to separate yourself from the pack is critical to your success.

While LinkedIn is terrific for finding a job online through personal networking, it is not always the place recruiters can easily find you. This is because some of these other resume sites have better SEO opportunities that are better integrated with Google. In fact, LinkedIn is so big, they are now a competitor of Google, and therefore both

Google and LinkedIn have battled for the hearts and minds of webs visitors. It seems smaller resume sites seem to get listed higher because they are not competitors in the big game, which is who controls the content of the Global Internet.

We have dedicated a full chapter to LinkedIn in Chapter 7: Getting LinkedIn Right, where you can read through my opinion on LinkedIn. Chapter 7 on LinkedIn has a ton of great tips and instructions on LinkedIn and what you need to be doing there. We only mention LinkedIn here because it is one of the top 10 resume/profile sites on the web and you must be listed there.

Ziprecruiter.com

Reason To Build Resume On ZipRecruiter: It's where headhunters roam. My experience has been that ZipRecruiter's own internal search for head-Hunters is excellent. I have been found as many times here as anywhere else online.

I had never heard of Zip Recruiter before I put my resume on there. One of the factors I would consider in getting on Zip Recruiter is they have a lot of headhunters who use them. Many headhunters are from overseas agencies. Headhunters are a subject I will cover later in this book. Zip Recruiter is a great place to get found by one. Zip Recruiter got me more agents contacting me than any other job site. You need to create an account on Zip Recruiter and post your resume.

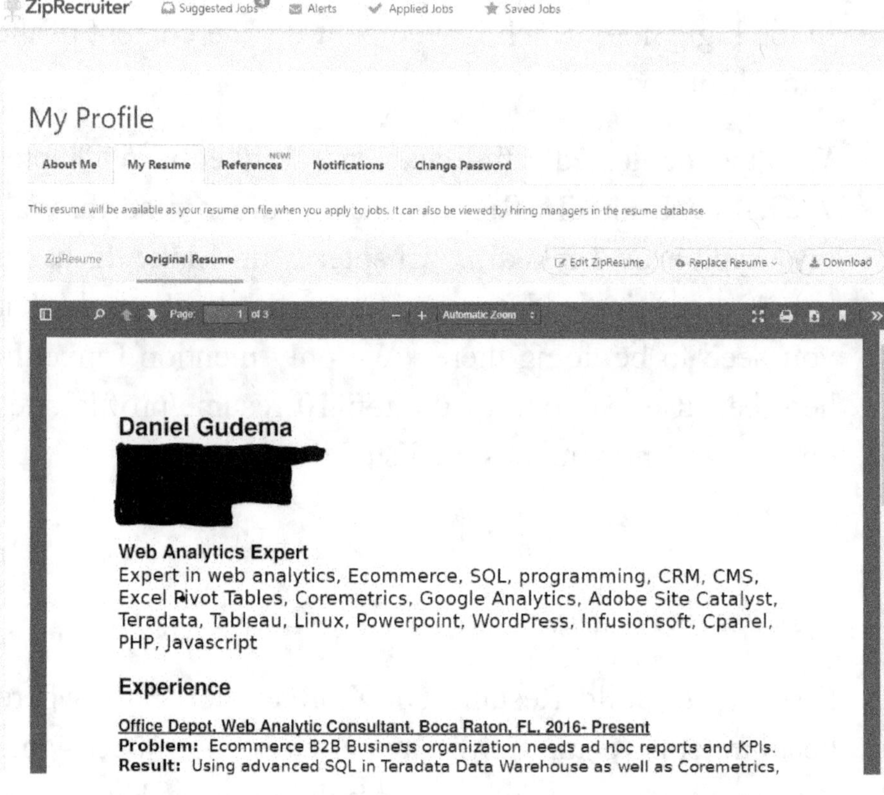

Notice on Zip Recruiter you can show your resume in its original form. That is a nice thing compared with all the resume profile builders. A lot of getting employers and head-hunters to notice you is how they perceive you fit into the job search parameters, which we can refer to as keywords or tagging.

Careerbuilder.com

Reason To Build Profile On CareerBuilder.com: Just like ZipRecruiter, I have found CareerBuilder.com resumes get searched by head-hunters. The only negatives it is virtual not used by employers directly.

You would think at this point Careerbuilder.com is pretty much a dead end and a very old job site, yet Careerbuilder.com has seen a big revival in its service selling access or data to headhunters in the form of resumes. So, like the other competitors, Careerbuilder.com has put some time and energy into making sure their resume upload functions well. This site is so well established that they compete with the likes of Indeed, yet have not kept up with all resume sites.

There is something to be said about the length of time a business like Careerbuilder.com and their domain name and business has been around. Age is used by Google as a way to meaure the importance of websites. What gives CareerBuilder its strength is a ton of inbound links on other websites in addition to the age of the site. Inbound links and tagging are SEO subjects you should get yourself a little bit acquainted with. The older established websites out there may be ugly like Craigslist, eBay or Pre-Dating.com, my own business, but they have the history and Google respects this history. That history makes it difficult for competitors to replace them.

Monster.com

Reason To Build Profile On Monster: A lot of young people are not aware of Monster's history. At one point in time they were the top job site, until job listings because irrelevant and resume listings became what is important. Their SEO has history and probably is the top back-links job site.

At one point in time Monster dominated the job search market online. It became the most well-known name in job searches. And the reason it was so successful is the branding   and   success   of   their   name.

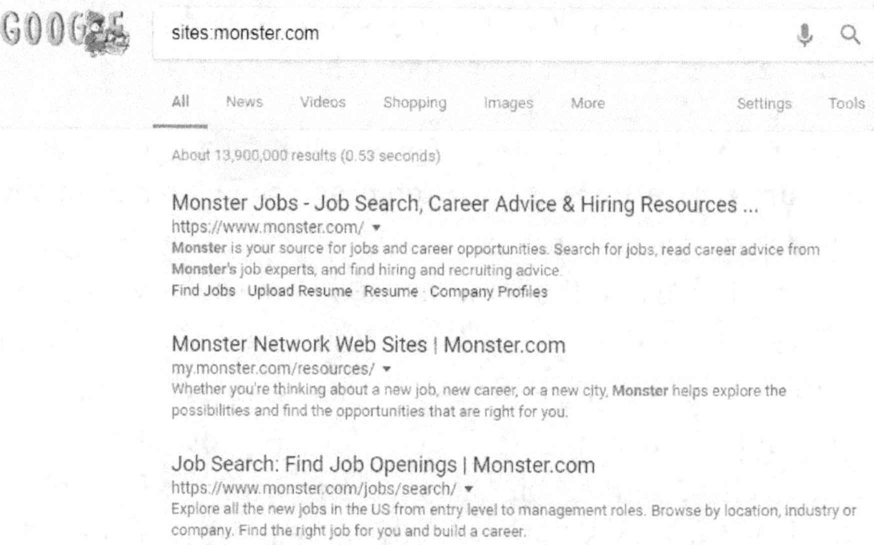

Notice that Monster.com appears on 13.9 Million web pages across the web. This is amazingly big. It means they are not going anywhere in terms of Google SEO.

I once heard the director of CareerBuilder speak in Miami around 2003 and he said no matter what CareerBuilder did in terms of TV advertising, Radio and online, people still thought of Monster when asked about job sites to turn to.

Today Monster is a shadow of its former self, but once again like CareerBuilder, Monster has seen its main business change from millions of visitors to become the seller of leads to headhunters. They have a sophisticated resume building engine and they have made uploading resumes a priority. You must be listed on Monster with your resume if you are looking for a job. It is critical to getting found online by head-hunters!

DICE.com

Reason To Place Resume On DICE: Back in the good old days of the Internet, DICE was the top place to find a job as a software developer and web designer. If you are a techie like me, then it is a must. And for non-techies, it is a unique place to be found.

When I was recently contacted by a headhunter I was kind of shocked when I asked him where he found me and my resume. The answer was DICE. This actually happened right as I was writing this chapter! If that is not an endorsement for DICE, I am not sure what is.

Skills

Top Skills	Experience	Last Used
Web Analytics	15+ years	Current
SQL Development	15+ years	Current
Javascript	13 years	Current
HTML	12 years	Current
Email Marketing	14 years	2014
Microsoft Excel	15+ years	Current
Microsoft PowerPoint	15+ years	Current
Microsoft Word	15+ years	Current
MySQL	15+ years	Current
Manager/Director Level Management	15+ years	Current

Because DICE is a skills-based website for techies they have a great tagging and categorization system. See the blue bars above.

Now DICE is probably the top technical job site out there. If you are not a programmer or part of the IT world you may not be acquainted with DICE. But now that you have, whether you are a programmer or an MBA guy like me, I now require you to add your resume to DICE. They do more than technical jobs and resumes. Even if you are in sales and marketing, if your company is within the tech industry, you may get found. In fact, if you are a marketing professional, you may have overlooked DICE or never heard of it. But as you can see from my experience it is quite effective in getting you found.

I would give DICE a lot of credit since they have been around for over 15 years and survived while a hundred job sites have come and gone long ago.

Glassdoor

Reason To Place Resume On Glassdoor: It's where every headhunter writes content about their company and manages reviews. You want to be on a website that has HR staff coming and going!

Most of you should know of Glassdoor as an employer review job site when it burst onto the scene around 2012 with a focus on reviews of corporations. Most know they have job listings by employers. What many people are not aware of is they also allow you to post your resume. It's a tremendously viewed site that gets well indexed on Google.   That means they come up in tons of searches. And I know for a fact that every HR department in America is all concerned about how they are viewed on Glassdoor, so that tells you quite a bit. The HR person who can get you in the door will be spending time on Glassdoor, writing content, updating photos, unlike Indeed or CareerBuilder. Glassdoor added the ability to upload and manage a resume on Glassdoor. That resume and profile area of Glassdoor is another important step in being found online. Just as a footnote, back in 2004, my future wife Linda and I built out Employerscorecard.com as a lark while working together. Employerscorecard.com is still around and is unchanged since 2004!

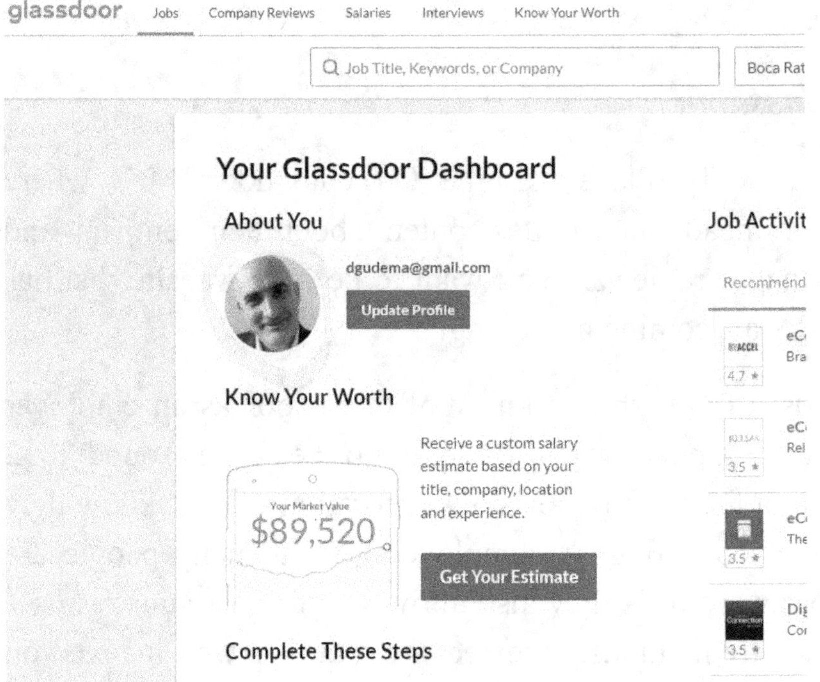

I added this Glassdoor Dashboard to show you how placing your photo into Glassdoor both humanizes you and makes the employer feel a connection with you. Notice I am happy and smiling. Luckily most of the employers and people I meet through my events and Linked connections say my photo is exactly as I appear. Authenticity is quite important!

Job.com

Reason To Build Profile On Job.com: In the brief time I spent on Job.com, I realized this is more of a lead gen for getting you to buy into resume creation and other third-party services. So, it really appeals to people who want to be serviced.

Because Job.com is really a lead gen system, I'm not going to get into exactly why you would want to be on it. It is pretty much the last couple of job sites you want to update. You never know who will find you on this site and as I have been saying in this book, you need to set the stage for getting found, and reducing your time searching for work. Getting this site's profile filled out is worth your time and energy.

Simplyhired.com

Reason To Build Profile On SimplyHired: SimplyHired is another job listing site with a resume builder and the more places you appear the great authority and SEO you personally have, so go for it!

Putting Together a Job Search Spreadsheet and Job Search Continuity.

It just happens that by mid-2016, I was getting so many

contacts for employment that I had to resort to using a spreadsheet to track every job I was applying for. It got to the point where I could not remember if I had applied for AT&T, Verizon, Black & Decker, Adobe or other Fortune 500 companies. These company names and contacts all turned into a blur to me because you are having the same conversation over and over again. And I was forgetting the names and headhunter contacts. You need to appear to whoever you are working with as capable and sincere. Remembering details like names and companies are part of this process.

Plus, when I was out of work again in the future, this was the best spreadsheet you can have imaginable because it lets you go right back to your employer contacts directly as well as to the special head-hunters with the corporate contracts. It was my ticket to getting rehired.

	A	B	C	D	E	F
					Talked	
					Around	Remote
		Company	Location	Title	Date	Allowed
1	1	PNC Bank	Pittsburgh	Senior Web Analyst	Oct 20?	Yes
2	2	Cisco	Raleigh	Senior Web Developer	3-Nov	Yes
3	3	Staples	Framingham	Senior Web Analyst		No
4	4	Office Depot	Boca Raton	Email Analyst		No
5	5	AT&T	Atlanta	Web Anaytics Architect		No
6	6	Verizon	Warren, N. Virg.	Web Analytics Consultant	20-Oct	No
7	7	Tmobile	Bothell	Web Analytics Consultant	15-Oct	No
8	8	Verizon	Piscataway	Senior Analyst/Manager	25-Oct	No
9	9	Echostar	Englewood	Adobe Analytics		No
10	10	Verizon Wireless	Irving Texas	Web Designer/Web Dev.		No
11	11	Alaskan Air	Tukwila, WA	Ecommerce Analyst	2-Nov	No
12	12	?	DC	Ecommerce Analyst		?
13	13	Walmart Labs	Sunnyvale	Web Analytics Consultant	15-Oct	No
14	14	CBS Sportsline	Fort Lauderdale	Data Engineer	1-Oct	
15	15	AutoNation	Fort Lauderdale	Web Analyst	3-Nov	
16	16	Adobe Systems (TCS)	San Jose	Web Analytic Consultant	5-Nov	
17	17	Home Depot	Atlanta	Web Analytic Manager	10-Nov	No
18	18	?	Orlando	Senior Web Analyst	10-Nov	
19	19	Stanley Black & Decker	Baltimore	Web Analytic Manager - Digital Marketing	Nov 2-Nov 12	No
20	20	CSAA (AAA)	Phoenix	Senior Web Analytics Data Analyst	14-Nov	Yes
21	21	TIAA	Charlotte	Senior Web Analyst	18-Nov	

As you can see, I am leaving off about 10 more columns with contact information, phone number, salary offer, a record if I had a call or meeting in person and notes about the company and if they had extended me an offer. This was my way of tracking everything and it was very important to my overall search. More importantly, notice the number and names of the companies I interacted with once I got my SEO well established.

As I sit here today finishing this book, I had recently ended a job and I was about to restart this search exactly where I had left off. This sheet is gold in the case of job search continuity. Otherwise, I would be starting from scratch and can't remember which company I had spoken with. Having a system like this in place can make a big difference in figuring out what company has contacted you in the past.

3

TOSS YOUR RESUME AND BRAND YOURSELF ONLINE

Who Are You?

Why should anybody read your blog articles, less your resume?

Can you be found in 3 clicks when employers search online?

Can you be found in 1 click when employers search online?

What makes you different than all the other guys online?

There is a sea of humanity out there online if you look up resumes and job candidates. Whatever field you are in, there are hundreds, if not thousands or millions that have a similar background. Some are living right down the street from you. You are competing with them every day for every job position. And if you look through the hundreds of similar resumes to yourself, like I have, they often have better schools they have attended, better job titles, better job descriptions and better accomplishments. In fact, they may actually all be better!

But are they?

Are they really better?

All you know is they have a better resume and ultimately better SEO.

If you really want to understand me personally, I get a little down when I read through these resumes. It can be overwhelming and it is a bit of downer to finally understand how many others out there on the streets that can do your job!

Wow, they must be as good as you or even better!

Or they may not be, but it does not matter who is better, what matters who gets found first, just like in normal Google Search Engine Optimization!

Am I as good as these other competitors? Who knows?

That feeling I have, that I am inferior, only lingers for a moment.

You have to really think about this sea of resumes you are competing with. Through Indeed.com, you can easily search across other people's resumes and see what the competition looks like.

These people are not just resumes showing up on the screen, they are all real people, your competitors and they will beat you out for a position if they can! But that's only if you let them!

If you don't get yourself together and change how you are competing, that great resume you see on Indeed is all headhunters and employers have to compare you with them. They may be the worst employee in real life, but on paper they are amazing! If they all look bigger and better, you need to consider remaking who you are, at least on paper and definitely online!

In a flat world, pre-Internet, where a stack of resumes is all that matters, you are one piece of paper stacked up with a thousand other people.

Anybody can look amazing on a resume. In fact, it is quite easy.

If you are not great at writing resumes, you can hire a person on Fiverr.com to make yourself sound and look better!

But there is a lot more to a job search than a resume in

this new online world order. You can get nicely SEO'd and found online today in ways that a simple resume cannot accomplish. If you compete simply in the flat world of the past, you are missing out on an additional 90% of job opportunities found online through SEO, social networking, community building, blogging and writing articles and other tools this book covers.

So obviously you need to find a way to not compete on just a resume. In fact, I say throw away your resume. I wish it were that easy. I almost say it because resumes are still the end all currency for employers. It is still a requirement at some point.

What you have to do is stop putting all your eggs in that one basket of a resume. Honestly, I would put a resume on a scale of 1 to 10 as a 5 in importance in finding a job. You need a resume right before you show up for an interview so they can use it to ask you questions about your past. A resume is an antique necessity but more so today an evil necessity, because it does not allow you to address a massive amount of the things that have worked for me personally that a resume cannot express out loud!

Remember, a resume is flat. But the world is no longer flat. The internet and online communities and tools are 3D. There are ways today to add your experience, opinion, leadership, and knowledge of the web and have employers view this.

So, if the resume is not the place to start, but rather a word doc or PDF you need to keep ready, where do you start your new career search?

In fact, the most important thing you should be thinking about and doing if you are unemployed at this point in time when you are undergoing a job search is ***Personal Brand Building***!

You need to consider your personal brand when looking for work.

What is your personal brand?

There have been a couple books written about branding yourself online, but they don't exactly cover the information that we are going to cover here in this book or in this chapter. They don't cover the tactics you will use to get your personal SEO level to the point where you will be found by employers. By finding, I mean the actual employers will call you and not just the head-hunters. Well, let's just say we will cover most of those items in this chapter now.

How do I know this personal branding technique will work?

I have found my last couple jobs by being called directly by employers! I was called out of the blue by employers or head-hunters representing employers who were looking for me. And by the time they had reached me, they knew things about me that no resume could teach them!

Names

In 2016 I wrote a book called *Names* under my name Dan Gudema, available on Amazon.com. *Names* was about choosing a brand and product name both online and offline.

So let's start with names. First off, is your personal name your brand? You need to decide if finding you is just your name or a full-blown corporate entity. There are reasons why you may want to be more than just you.

Deciding on your personal branding is an important aspect we will get into, because I decided in 2014, around the time I created a startup pitch event, where I built my personal community, to come up with a brand name. That brand name was specific to the events I was running and the career goals I was aiming for. My brand was called StartupPOP. It was organically created. That means the name rose up from within the project I was working on as a natural evolution. That is how the world should work.

I was under pressure to come up with a business name because the shark-tank like events we were running in Boca Raton, Florida needed to finally collect funds. So I incorporated. That is a reason to come up with a name.

But the business name was more than that. StartupPOP I realized was a name that I could use for my personal social media and a way to get recognition and grow my community. I could not just run events called Dan Gudema. I could, but it would not make any sense!

But let's get to the really important question.

Why do you need an online brand name?

This book is about personally SEO'ing yourself online, getting found in the Google search engine and other job site results and how to do it. Overall you are connected to your online brand and online brands are what people remember, follow, connect, tweet and Google ultimately indexes well.

I could have remained Dan Gudema on Twitter, but I renamed it at some point StartupPOP as well. I could have made all my blogs Dan Gudema's blog. I could have just used my name. And for some that works great. It's more a matter of what you what to accomplish.

Let's just say this, are you going to call your blog the same name as your name?

Do you understand what I am saying about brand vs. your name?

Are you the brand?

If you are not the brand, then you need to create one.

You may be asking yourself, why do I need to brand myself online? The answer is simple. Your brand is part of your plan to get yourself so well SEO'd you get found automatically by employers, other thought leaders, your followers and the Global Internet. That is part of switching your career search from push to pull. You need to pull in the employers as well as the head-hunters and not be pushing out your resume. They need to be able to find you however they can and that is where you can make the biggest difference in how not only are you found, but how you are personally perceived! Remember, you are who you want to be online.

If you are going to blog you need a brand and your name personally is not a brand exactly (though it could be if you are famous!). In a later chapter, we are going to discuss the how and why on the technical creation of your own blogs and some of the best places to place your blog articles.

If you read this book carefully you will know long before you write a single word in your blog why you are doing the blogging, where to blog, what to blog and how to do the blogging to get the biggest bang for your buck and get found!

We are going to get into community and SEO tech and SEO text at some point in this book, and that is where this brand name becomes important.

Notice word the "Startup" in the name StartupPOP I chose as my brand.

That was intentional.

Just as important, I want to cover my name theory from my book *Names* if you are trying to brand yourself. My name theory behind all names are the same, whether it is a blog, a website, a product, a company, Twitter, Facebook or other mediums, like Medium.com.

There are 4 things you need to discover in a name. By discover I mean they typically can occur naturally in a name. You just need to look and find them. You can accomplish 1 of these points or up to 4 of these points in coming up with a brand name. If you come up with all 4 points, you have an amazing great brand name. Hit 2 or 3 points and the name is good enough!

Is The Name Memorable?

Memory is a natural process that seems to happen in the brain. People can either instantly remember a name or they can't. And there is little science I can give you, other than can they remember the name in 30 seconds, 10 minutes, hours and days. If they can't the name is just not that memorable. Just remember that memorable names are most important. If you want more info about names buy my book *Names*! I have come up with brand names like Oops I'm Single, Gum Chucks, What's Up Car and StartupPOP.

Is The Name Familiar?

Familiar simply means it is a name people will say they think they remember hearing in the past when they have never heard it before. The reason What's Up Car sounds familiar is it is similar to WhatsApp, a popular social media app.

Does The Name Have Personality?

By personality, I mean a name can be funny, have a sense of quirkiness like Go Daddy or just be original in the way it sounds. This is opposed to non-original or generic sounding. Years ago I heard the manager of CareerBuilder complain that no matter what they did people always remembered Monster, the big career site at the time. Why? Monster has personality.

Can You Tell What It Is About?

This is the oldest reason for brand names of all reasons. If you can tell what industry it is in or something that gives you a hint it will help the name and help overall.

The best names do all of these things, but they at least have to do 1 or 2. Names without 1 of 4 points are just wrong.

Not all names are perfect, but from a branding standpoint, memorability is the number one point. If you can't get people to remember the name, you are less likely to make the name work as a brand, get repeat visitors, and get them to remember the name or have a solid brand.

4

CREATE YOUR OWN ONLINE COMMUNITY

What is your own online community?

Better yet, what is a community?

Everybody pretty much is a member of a community and understands what one is, but do you have your own. By your own, I mean specifically a community that revolves around you and/or your brand. This chapter discusses why you need to build your own online community, the impact of being found online and your career and how to build an online community if you have not already started.

Everybody knows what a community is. You may be a member of 1 or many communities. Less of us are members of a real organized community than ever before. When I was a kid we were a member of a block of friends and families that would come together for at least dinners and hanging out. That was one community I belonged two. We were also a member of a Jewish religious community in Morristown, NJ where we had a local rabbi and leader. My high school was a community. I was on a soccer team that was a community. I was heavily involved with B'nai B'rith Youth Group which was a community. I was in a fraternity called Tau Epsilon Phi in college that was a community. There are probably several forms of a community you are a member of. The most important part of this is that they get organized and that community encourages people to interact, learn and connect personally. But there really is something special you remember about all your past communities. It was the human interaction that you will never forget, because our childhood communities typically are part of who we are today. That is what you are looking for online. And it's out there on the web.

You already know about your community, your HOA, your school district, your city, your county and your government, civic, political or religious community. In some cases, people join groups and organizations, both religious and non-religious to join a community.

What is the big difference between those naturally occurring communities and your personal community?

It is simple. Your community is one you nurtured to follow you and not just a typical organization, government, school or religious affiliation. It is actually a community that you manage and interacts with and when you need it for your personal business use. It is there for you to take advantage of when you need help in finding a job, getting gigs or making a living.

Do the members really understand it is your community?

The answer to whether or not they understand it is your community, has more to do with branding, conceptually what they get out of it and how it impacts them. If it has no impact, it really is not useful to that community.

You need to think through what value you provide to your community. What can you offer that means something more than just a guy trying to collect emails or Facebook friends? Why follow you?

Just like those other typical communities you are a member of, they all use ways to communicate from newsletters to social media and to community meetings.

I went to a one-day seminar in Fort Lauderdale a couple years ago to listen to a speaker named Bill Walsh who really focused on the concept of community building. What he said, and I was already in the middle of this, is setting up your personal social media and other online communities and offline events was a way to build your community. He mentioned that you need to start building this community long in advance of your end goal. If you want to start a new career long term, you need to start gathering connections on places like LinkedIn. If you want to start a new business and have early loyal followers, it starts with your inner circle. How do you get an inner circle? You start by building a community. I hope you are starting to understand that communities are built anywhere online.

If you were to wait till the day you lost your current job to start building your community or the first day of the start of a business you would be for months, if not years be behind on community building you needed to have been doing all those years in advance.

The answer is to start building your community today for whatever you want to do tomorrow!

We have been connecting and creating relationships online since the very beginning in tools like Compuserve, Prodigy, and AOL.

Back in the beginning of the Internet emails and a person's contact list was the first place people connected. The problem with this was emails are one to one connections.

Being able to create a group and manage that group became the next level of community available for online visitors.

A very early Internet community application was called Geocities. I remember we all homesteaded, what we called it back then, grabbing a virtual online space. That space was the beginning of a series of applications and systems that would transform online connecting and ultimately lead to social networking and social media.

When Facebook was first introduced, I noticed Facebook introduced the concept of "Follow" and that was the beginning of large-scale connecting. We could keep a couple hundred if not thousands or millions connected to us and nurture our online community every day, every moment.

Eventually, online community building evolved into segmented social networking for business, personal and other. There are differences between where you build your community. But in the end, it may sound backward; I have found the best community building is in the old fashion in-person meeting. That is the tried and true place that people get together and network and meet. But what is different about the world of in-person networking today is you can easily put together an event that draws people in with little to no cost. That's because the tools online are crazy good at connecting the right people to the right event today. And many people are more used to being invited to events on a regular basis.

I have to give Meetup and Eventbrite a lot of credit for creating a "Marketplace" for creating and managing events online before these tools appeared. That was the issue at the beginning of running in-person events. Using these two tools alone, I have drawn in thousands of people to attend my events held in Boca Raton, Florida.

Meetup and Eventbrite are the best social media, social networking, and social event tools in your arsenal. Learn to use them and take advantage of their Google SEO power!

So, while there are well-known social media tools like LinkedIn, Twitter, Facebook, Pinterest and Instagram out there, Meetup and Eventbrite have more potential to get you to the top of the Google listings than any social media tools.

Social event tools are more important in terms of both online and offline functionality than all those well-known ones! In fact, Meetup and Eventbrite can do one thing for you that no other social media tool can do. They can push your event to the top of Google searches almost immediately. They are so highly indexed with Google and are coded so well, they are pure SEO indexed content. That's because these are "timely", "local" and "relevant".

Google content that contains dates gets indexes as important and higher in the rankings. An example would be "Web Analytics Meetup – November 27, 2017, 6 pm – The Greenhouse – Boca Raton, FL." That content is Google gold.

Google content that is focused on a local geographic place gets indexed higher in the rankings for local users. An example would be "Boca Raton, FL 33434". Just these cities, states and zip codes in your content have an impact on Google rankings. So getting your event onto Google is a big deal for Google search if you get it right. This is one of those secrets of getting found online. You need to also understand that getting found multiple ways is important. It is not all about job sites. The future for finding workers will be AI based and use social media and intelligent searching. You need to prepare for that day now.

Google content that is relevant and focused on a specific subject people look up gets indexed higher in the rankings. An example would be "Web Analytics Meetup". An event about Web Analytics would get ranked well locally. That means that your content could end up on page 1! That is also Google gold.

GO SEO YOURSELF TIP # 1

USE A CLOUD-BASED SYSTEM FOR SEO, AND NOT JUST YOUR OWN WEBSITE

Meetup and Eventbrite are such amazing SEO opportunities because they utilize geography and events, two of the top content types Google loves. By setting up your own Meetup group and Eventbrite events you will be able to get to the top of searches locally for your brand within hours and minutes and not days! But think about what I am saying. I am saying to you, create a Meetup group that is all about what you know or your expertise. That means being a leader and creating the group and nurturing and managing the group.

I mention throughout this book I will take you out of your comfort zone. Trust me, I want to be home on a Wednesday night each month watching Game of Thrones reruns on HBO or my college basketball team, The University of Maryland. I want to just sit on the couch and veg out or spend times with my young boys. But I still go out and run events. I have done this consistently from the beginning of my job apocalypse, and guess what... it has been a major breakthrough for me. It combines networking with building amazingly great SEO for myself.

I have noticed over the years how many people tell me they read my bio on Meetup. See that bio above in this image that tells people about me. That little bio is what

SEO online is all about. The event attendees were drawn into the Meetup group because of their interest in a subject, like startups. Then they read the content and finally, they read about me.

The amount of time and energy I put into these events was considerable. And like everything else in this book the results were not always instant, but they did produce results.

Most overnight successes took a long time to succeed. It's a general fact of life that most endeavors require you to work hard and long with the personal faith that you will see the end results.

Another important point about building your own online community is everything else we talk about in this book will feed into your community, whether it is social media, LinkedIn, your footer in your emails, your press releases, and your communications in general. You have to have a place, a center for your personal communications. For some, it is a personal website. We will get into a personal website and how that can really succeed with blogging. For some, it will be LinkedIn as the center of their community.

Many claim Facebook as the center of their community. I will comment on Facebook in this book. I have an opinion and my opinion is it is not good for finding work. In fact, please somebody write to me and tell me how you found a job using Facebook! For the task at hand, Facebook may play a significant role in community building, but it is not exactly where I recommend starting when it comes to your career. That's because Facebook may be good at connecting many people together who have the same genes, high school, college or club, but Facebook is not so good at helping employers find employees. In fact, it may be where they see you holding a joint in a picture and decide to move onto another candidate!

Meetup

The best place I have found online for community building for my career has been Meetup. Let's get into why Meetup has beat out all these other social media, including the great and mighty Facebook. It's simple. Meetup is the best place to attract local community members. And at the same time, since I have built software as a developer, I would not say it is the best technical system, nor does it have amazingly cool features or user interfaces.

Meetup is quite ordinary and in some cases confusing. But being a great technical system does not matter. What matters is it gives you the results you desire and need. Meetup has millions of categorized members. Meetup has such good SEO on Google that they will find people to join your group and attend your event. Let me preface this with it is business and career focused as opposed to Facebook. That's a general concept I want you to remember as you consider a dozen other options for community building. Within hours of posting an event on Meetup, your event may show up on Google at the top of the listings using your SEO keywords, which in my case has been "startup events", "pitch events" and "finding venture capital".

GO SEO YOURSELF TIP #2

KNOW YOUR SEO KEYWORDS

A lot of people don't realize SEO is composed of placing keywords into website content that gets indexed by search engine keywords. If you know your keywords and use them appropriately in the right situations online, like in the title, content, extra pages and other parts of your Meetup, your listing will get easily found by Google, which means people will find

you!

Meetup has built the necessary tools to allow you to easily and cheaply communicate to your community of members. You can actually send to a single email address and hit your group up with a quick message, which is a complete time saver and ultimately a major leapfrog in how cloud-based online sites in the past worked. I can send a message to 10,000 people right now in 30 seconds using Meetup.

Eventbrite

The next best place for community building events is Eventbrite for attracting people to your community. It is great for SEO, but Eventbrite has not taken up the cause of community building. Eventbrite does not help you build online groups that work together with your personal team. Eventbrite has a goal to be a competitor of Ticketmaster, where they fill whole stadiums and make a ton of money doing it. Their focus is not yours in this case because what I have found with Eventbrite is you pretty much have to start your community over from scratch per event. That a real negative. So, just send them to Meetup or Facebook.

Then there is Twitter, Instagram, and Pinterest. These are simply interactive press release services. Twitter, Instagram, and Pinterest are for communicating to people about your message. These services are less personal and less community oriented. Only in a handful of cases over the years have I used Twitter as a way to build meaningful relationships. Yet I have sent thousands of Tweets. I think I had 10 personal chat interactions in 10 years. What is important is providing a link back to get them to join your community whether it is on Meetup or LinkedIn   or   elsewhere.

The Almighty Facebook

Facebook would seem like the best place for community building, but your work community is probably not your parents and friends. Your work community are the people you connect with in YOUR industry. That's a big difference with friends and family. Some people may wholeheartedly disagree with me about Facebook and community building because it is a community building gargantuan website. But my experience has been that Facebook has a lot of negatives for business purposes and can cross the line between business and personal. There is a line in the sand and you need to recognize it. I have seen local groups successfully use Facebook as a way to build their personal community, but once again there is too much bleeding between personal and business. You need to know the difference! In fact, even if they were successful in building a business community on Facebook, it rarely impacts finding a job. That is what this book is about.

When it comes to Facebook you may find out the hard way for many reasons why it is not great for business purposes and getting hired. For instance, all your crappy non-business pictures can expose you there to your dirty camping trips and drunken moments when other people post pictures about you. It's really important to control your message and your image and Facebook just has too much vulnerability when it comes to managing how you appear. Don't get this concept wrong! I mention over and over again in this book, how you have to take the right approach to each online service. They are not all equal.

Leaving Facebook for family and friends may be why you will venture out of the great and wonderful Facebook and move on to where the people who hire people hang out, like on LinkedIn! That is where you need to be!

5

<u>MASTER THE TASK!</u>

If you can master the tech, you can master the text and master the task!

Learn how to communicate online!

What do I mean by communicating online?

If you want to succeed at any of these online SEO tasks we mention in this book, you need to be a great communicator. And being able to communicate can mean writing, video or audio or a combination of all three in certain cases. Communicating is how employers and headhunters find you. The better you communicate the more chances you will be a candidate for being hired. There is much more to communicating than simply LOL or texting.

Master The Tech

But before you can be a great communicator you need to know how online tools and systems work. This means you need to be able to learn systems quickly. You need to be able to login to a new system like the online job sites, the backend of Google Analytics, Meetup or other third party systems and become a guru ASAP! A great example for me in the past year is I had to become an expert at Amazon SellerCentral, the place you go to sell Amazon products for my employer. Let's just say that Amazon is a complete mess when it comes to their backend. Unlike their carefree easy to use e-commerce site, with things like Prime and one-click shopping, the back-end of Amazon is like an old building with a thousand add-ons, and nobody has refurbished the place since 1999.

Meanwhile, Amazon is highly respected and does a great job converting sales. Over $168 billion e-commerce dollars were spent by consumers on Amazon in 2017, close to 50% of online e-commerce. They are fat and happy on the back side. In fact, I realized that without a class or someone holding your hand showing you what to do on Amazon SellerCentral, it is quite confusing compared to an ecommerce solution like Shopify.

Honestly most online websites and systems today should be easy to learn. They should work for you and be simple from the moment you create an account. You should intuitively know what to do next and everything should be easy. That's not how the world works. Sometimes these systems are not just hard to figure out; they have tons of features you will never be aware of. I was recently explaining to people you can download all the email addresses of your LinkedIn contacts. Most people don't know that and to do it, it is confusing.

When website companies like Amazon have fewer competitors, the cost of change and pressure to fix things and make them better lessons. Yes, there are amazingly easy things to work with like Instagram for instance, but there are still a dozen systems I can name out there, including LinkedIn, that are still not very user-friendly in my opinion. It's all an opinion!

You need to expect the world to be not so user-friendly. Therefore, do not go to any new online website with high expectations. You never know what to expect and don't freak out when you realize the system has been built by tech guys not marketers or UI people. I have freaked out. But then I calmed down and started to learn it.

You need to be able to learn everything, quickly. For instance, the help and FAQ wording can be completely incorrect or the way it works can go against standards. Meetup, which I can tell you with complete honesty, has one of the worst UI's I have ever worked with. UI stands for User Interface. In the end, you need to master it, whatever it is. I ended up mastering Amazon SellerCentral. It was a pain in the butt, but with a bunch of Youtube videos, you get yourself trained and slowly you develop an expertise. Everybody goes right to Youtube these days. If you are having a problem, start on Youtube with overviews!

Master The Text

In discussing how you should write and communicate online, I could write a whole book about how to do it. The communications place I am referring to is any place you can communicate with written content or personal writing, from writing your resume to writing your bio to writing emails, Tweets, and blogging. For you, they need to be perfect, if possible. I don't tolerate spelling errors, incorrect information, run on sentences or other mistakes. Nobody tolerates it. Whatever you do, never make a spelling error. It is so easy online to check your spelling and make sure words are spelled correctly, that you should never ever spell anything wrong. Yet I see spelling errors everywhere.

Sometimes we are moving so fast we make mistakes. I don't want to, but I do. If I had to make a decision between speed and perfection, I would take speed every time and make a few mistakes here and there. And probably most of you reading are in the same boat as me. But, we all should make sure that our communications with the world are as clear as we can make it, about yourself and about your subject matter. Some of us are great communicators and some are not. If you are not, then get a book and start to study the art of communications.

GO SEO YOURSELF TIP #3

BE REPETITIVE AND CONSISTENT IN YOUR COMMUNICATIONS

Within any of your writing online, it is important to repeat your keywords, the words used to find you often and repeat them. To become an authority and get found on Google, it is critical that Google believes and measures how authoritative you are for SEO. Make sure you have specific words embedded repeatedly throughout your titles, posts, and content. My keywords were "Web Analytics" because that is the field I was working in at the time I wrote this book.

There are really two levels of writing you need to choose between when writing on the Internet. And both of these levels of writing are acceptable depending on where you are writing. One is AP style and the other is natural language. As you can see I have written this book in natural language. By writing natural language I write as I would speak. That's because this book has been written in the first person. I want you, the reader, to feel like I am writing about you and to you directly. That is the method I recommend you use in your Internet-based writing. The important part of this is making sure you write about the reader and to the reader. It can't be all "me and I" words. It needs to be "you" words. What I do is go back to my blogs and read it carefully and try to remove the I's and ME's and see if I can replace them with YOU.

Within your communications, you need to be a teacher and authority, not a self-serving person. If you were to start a Meetup about your expertise, you need to make sure your writing is inclusive and helps people feel they will get something out of the meeting. That is really important in how you communicate.

The ability to communicate effectively applies to all aspects of communicating online from websites, blogging, social network postings, landing pages, squeeze pages, push notifications and email communications. It includes videos you create for Youtube and anyplace you can communicate a message online.

The only way to improve your ability to communicate is practice, practice, practice. And by practice, I don't mean writing in a physical journal. With the web there is no need for practice, you just have to go out and do it. That is why we blog, not just to get traffic and SEO but to get better at writing in general.

The same is true for video and audio. Creating a Youtube video or Podcast just requires going out and figuring it out and doing it. Just a recommendation, I use a program called Screen-Cast-O-Matic for creating my videos!

Master The Task

If you want to be an expert at something I have found it is best to teach it. While you are teaching a subject you are forced to be an expert. That is why I enjoy teaching a class on web analytics almost once a semester at a local college. It allows me to do research for the class on the subject matter and get up to speed on the subject.

To master a specific subject you become the authority.

GO SEO YOURSELF TIP #4

BEING AN AUTHORITY MOVES YOU HIGHER UP IN SEO.

Becoming an authority on a subject is what drives our personal SEO higher online. The terms we often use in SEO will move us to the top of the Google search engine listings if we continue to work on being an authority in many ways on many websites. Websites become authorities on subjects because of a combination of keywords, inbound links, a long history and relevant content. Become an authority on a subject and you will show up higher in the listings.

6

<u>GET LINKEDIN RIGHT!</u>

I have decided to spend a whole chapter just on LinkedIn because it is such a critical part of getting yourself SEO'd correctly online. There are whole books you can read just about getting LinkedIn set up correctly. I would not just buy that one book and just focus on LinkedIn. That would be short-sighted. In fact, I have been contacted for jobs 90% of the time not from LinkedIn. There are so many other online places to get set up for your online persona and SEO and head-hunters know that. That is why they are not just ON LinkedIn. Yet LinkedIn is an absolute must for looking for work online and self-promoting yourself. It is really more of a reputation and communications site for finding a job than a resume finder site. Everybody checks your profile out, but few find you there!

We will cover in this chapter everything you need to be doing on LinkedIn. Most of you hopefully have already put hours, days, months and years building out your LinkedIn profile. I see at least most of my ex-coworkers put the time in to get the basics in place. But being just average on LinkedIn is not enough. You want to be in the top 1% to succeed with LinkedIn. Being in the top 1% is a tall order because one of the little secrets to LinkedIn is popularity. Popular people, culturally and those who are on Tedx or have a best seller or even better, have created a billion-dollar company have instant clout on LinkedIn. You are competing with these popular figures. I use the word competing because you have to look at yourself as a media product online. You are the product.

GO SEO YOURSELF TIP #5

COMMUNICATE ABOUT YOUR SUBJECT IN LONG FORM, NOT JUST POSTS

Stop viewing yourself as a simple resume online. You are so much more. You need to start selling yourself, your brand and your product, which is YOU! Take every opportunity you have to write blogs on LinkedIn and other sites like Medium and comment on everything you can because what they say in the PR business is any news is good news. That means when you post a comment

on a LinkedIn article, your name (or personal brand) gets exposure. If you are reading this book online, go right into LinkedIn and make a comment now! Find my last article and leave me a comment!

So, where do we start with LinkedIn, since there is so much to cover? Let's start with the basics. You need to get your LinkedIn to 99 percent complete. And you need to get your LinkedIn to the point where it is so filled out and well-rounded that an employer will feel compelled to contact you.

Let's break down LinkedIn into 5 areas of focus. This way of splitting up SEO based LinkedIn tasks, let's you know what to focus on. It will determine not just where to start but rather where to shore it up. But first, you have to do an assessment using our list to determine if you are already doing a great job or missing elements that we recommend below.

Whether you think you have the perfect LinkedIn profile or not, you will get out of this chapter a couple more tidbits of improvement recommendations. You will quickly see what you are great at on LinkedIn and what you are not doing on LinkedIn. That will quickly become obvious to you and it's very easy to fix.

What is important for you personally in terms of SEO is not exactly what is important for LinkedIn. LinkedIn tries to steer you in a direction to help you with your % complete. LinkedIn profile recommendations uses a concept called Poke Yoke. Poke Yoke is a Japanese word for little sayings that get you motivated to do what a business wants you to do like throw away your garbage at McDonald's.

Are those Poke Yoke recommendations by LinkedIn really what you need to be doing or are they what they need you to be doing to build THEIR business? You have to prioritize your work in LinkedIn based on what will have the greatest impact for you, not LinkedIn. Notice how LinkedIn always wants to access your email list and send out LinkedIn invites. Is that good for you personally? Maybe yes, maybe no.

Here are the areas you need to focus on in order to optimize your LinkedIn profile for SEO, starting in this order.

1. SEO Profile Title Wording
2. Writing LinkedIn Updates, Articles and Comments
3. LinkedIn Visualizations
4. LinkedIn SEO Tagging
5. Increasing and Building Your LinkedIn Community

Notice that we break these 5 tasks down by SEO based categorizations. In the world of SEO, certain things will have an impact that is greater for you. And when it comes to SEO, there are different types of optimizations that are not going to result in higher Google results. They will result in better and more impactful actions by those other people on LinkedIn in noticing you, adding you as a LinkedIn contact or contacting you with a message.

GO SEO YOURSELF TIP #6

ONLINE COURTEOUSNESS AND KINDNESS ARE REWARDED IN KIND

Whether on Linked or any other interactive social networking platforms always respond to a comment, contact or message with a reciprocal message. This increases your authority among the person interacting with you and it's just good form. When somebody says hey I want to let you know that we have a new marketing service that you should be aware of and puts in a LinkedIn request, you should respond. I know that they are trying to solicit me for a project. My inclination is to ignore these people, but I also know it is important to engage. I typically accept their invitation and then let them know that we are not right now considering a third party but will keep them in mind. Be good, be kind and be courteous. You never know when you will need this contact.

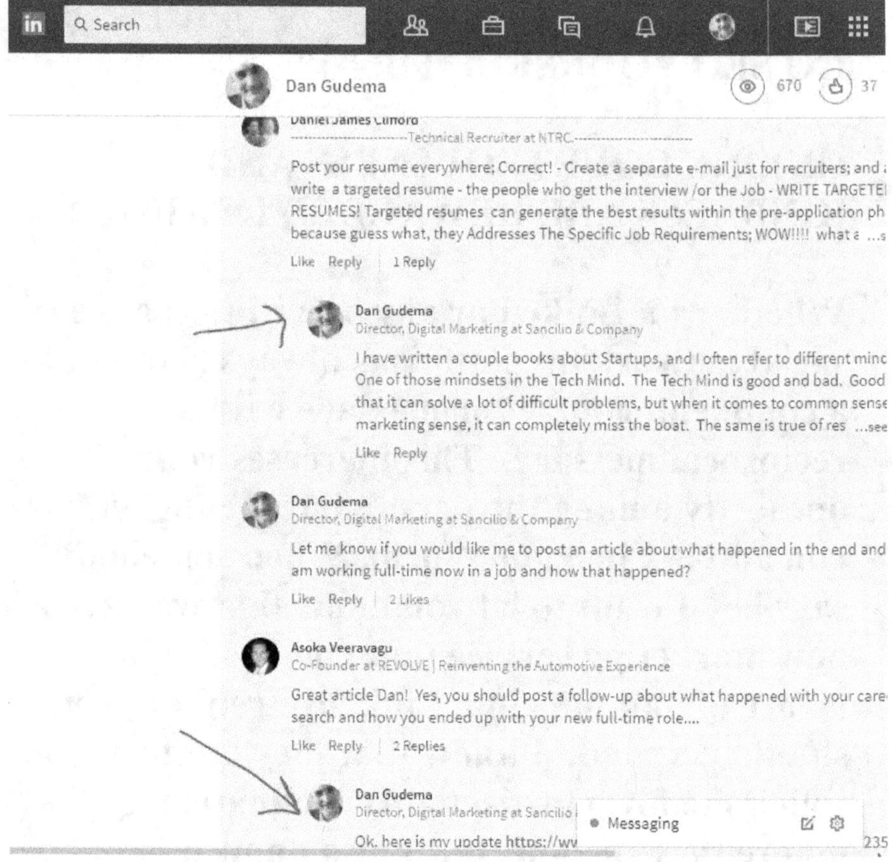

Notice in the article above that I consistently replied to all the comments made in the article I wrote.

#1 SEO Profile Wording

Let's face it, the most important SEO impact, and pretty much the only part of LinkedIn that will be available for SEO on Google will be the very topline profile text that shows up on Google. All the other parts of your LinkedIn listing and profile are important, but the profile summary is most important for getting found and noticed on Google. This means your name and your title and a few elements will be the only parts of LinkedIn that will be present on Google.

GO SEO YOURSELF TIP #7

WHAT PEOPLE CAN SEE ON GOOGLE SEARCH RESULTS IS VERY IMPORTANT TO CLICK-THROUGH RATES

For SEO purposes and SEO planning, there are really two objectives. The first is to get indexed well on Google and show up at the top of the listings when people search. But second to that is the wording that shows up. For many cloud-based services that get indexed with our information like LinkedIn, we can generally control the wording that visually shows on Google and optimize our Google search results to attract people to click on our Google search results listing. CTR (Click Through Rate) is the percentage of people who click on our Google search result page.

The Importance of LinkedIn Summary Content.

Take a look at this Google listing of my LinkedIn profile when I search for my name on Google:

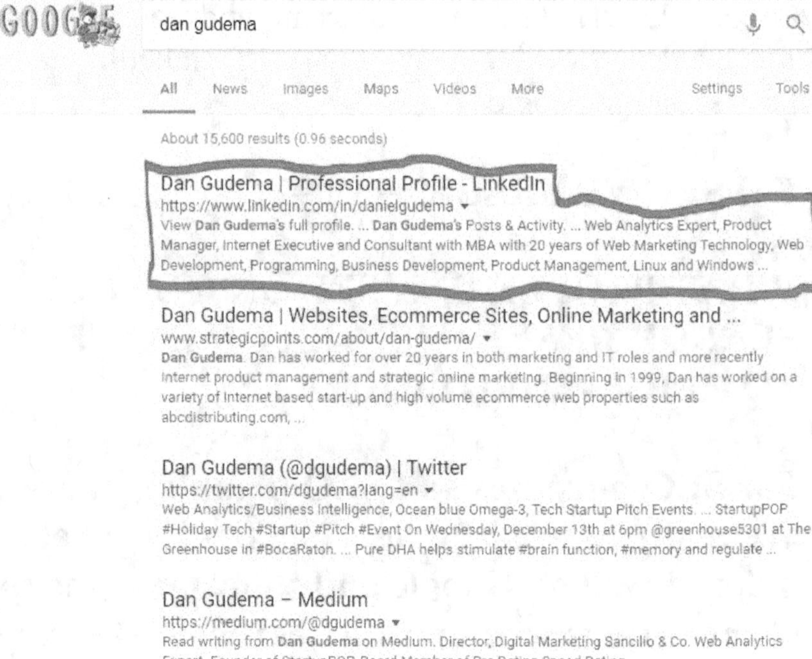

If you look carefully what gets indexed from your profile's LinkedIn page text and seen on Google are your name and the first 214 characters from your written profile summary. The summary is the most important LinkedIn SEO part.

Notice that my actual title, name, university, city, and state do not get listed. Here is the actual wording that my profile summary starts with:

"Web Analytics Expert, Product Manager, Internet Executive and Consultant with MBA with 20 years of Web Marketing Technology, Web Development, Programming, Business Development, Product Management, Linux, and Windows"

So, it is really important to notice that I put the most searchable targeted SEO words into the LinkedIn Summary.

#2 Writing LinkedIn Updates, Articles and Comments

As you have been reading this book, hopefully, you have picked up on the fact that your keywords are very important in getting found and getting indexed. Unlike the job profile on LinkedIn, which is more about visually getting read by an employer, the articles they let you write on LinkedIn actually do get indexed by Google.

Because you can write these articles and produce content on LinkedIn and get higher in the SEO listing and authority, articles or blogging on LinkedIn is for me the greatest source of value I can take advantage of on LinkedIn. It does not hurt that writing is my thing.

We talk a lot about becoming an expert and authority on subjects. That is really the bottom line of having a career. Writing an article is a way to get yourself higher up in the minds of employers as an expert. However, you have to bring original content and thought to a piece of writing or the people you are trying to influence will ignore your article.

My experimenting with writing articles that are not relevant to my career and my community as well as my keywords have not done that well. When articles really hit home for readers in a way that makes them connect with you personally, that is the type of article you want to write.

Articles you write about personal truth and personal experience are what get read the most online. This is something a lot of people on LinkedIn fear writing!

But thought leadership is not about being liked or holding in all your thoughts. You have to lay it all out on the line every once in a while to make an impact.

GO SEO YOURSELF TIP #8

WRITE FINDABLE CONTENT IN ARTICLES THAT NEED TO BE READ!

It is important to make sure your blog articles are content rich and hit the right keywords when Google's search bots reach your site and suck in all the words, categories and tags. That information is critical to getting found.

Your goal with writing a LinkedIn article is to get to a subject that is findable through a common Google search as well as readers desiring the content. And believe it or not, you have to think about challenging readers assumptions about the world. That means often using titles that are the opposite of what you really mean to get the reader started. I wrote an article called "Why I

Would Never Hire A Startup Person!" on LinkedIn. Before I could get tons of hate mail, the readers realized immediately that I was sarcastic and meant the opposite. And yes, it was well received.

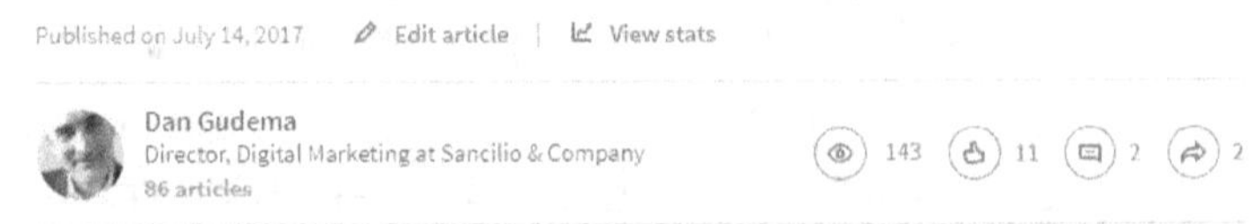

Published on July 14, 2017   Edit article | View stats

Dan Gudema
Director, Digital Marketing at Sancilio & Company
86 articles

143   11   2   2

This article will talk about a significant change that has already started in how Fortune 500 and Corporations hire people. What used to be a sacred cow is now quite common. What is it? It's quite simple. It's the Startup Generation vs. Traditional Corporate Workers. Ex-Startup people will and are competing for corporate jobs every day. I know, I was one of them.

Millions of millennials set out to create a startup or consulting firm as their first job after college, or forget college altogether. I remember the Yahoo Finance Article around 2004 that said skip college and grad school and just create a startup. Back then I argued that was dumb advice. Some have proved me wrong. But even the people who did not prove me wrong and tried, tried, tried and failed at a startup are by far better off for their experience. Trust me. What they experienced and went through was a ring of fire and they learned stuff that no corporate job could teach you. And as this Startup Generation continues to jump into $16,000 12-week code schools to learn Python and R, we will have more and more of what I call the "Startup Generation" eventually applying for real jobs. It is actually a career path! And one that makes total sense.

This article comes from the 100 articles I have written on LinkedIn. Please visit my LinkedIn profile if you would like to read my articles!

One of my mentors, Michael O'Donnell told us he wrote a wildly successful article entitled "Why I Would Never Accept Your LinkedIn Request!" It got thousands of views because it was quite controversial. It spoke about the kinds of people that he would never connect with and why and ultimately he connected with tons of new people because of the article.

#3 *LinkedIn Visualizations*

This is a funny story I tell, but I was determined to make my LinkedIn profile appear to viewers and potential employers that I was an expert in web analytics. Let's just say I am an expert, but there was something about my profile that was not saying I am an expert. It was the background image. I was in the middle of a job search and I ended up placing the following background image in my LinkedIn profile in order to show stats and graphs in the background to enhance who I was:

What was amazing is about 30 minutes after I updated

this graphical image onto my LinkedIn profile page I was contacted immediately by a potential employer. He told me he had seen my LinkedIn profile and was impressed. I never told him I had just updated my background image. And maybe the background image was not the real reason he contacted me. But it was so serendipitous that I believed it was that background image which made the difference. And yes I did get the job!

Your Picture on LinkedIn

A couple times in this book I mention that you need to update your photo and make sure your photo shows you in the best light (literally) you can be. That means the photo should reflect upon you personally. You should be consistent and use the same photo everywhere. It should show you as positive with a smile and energetic. Trust me, a bad photo never gets you an advantage over another job candidate, but a great photo showing you as positive is more likely going to get you contacted. I don't believe at least on LinkedIn or any resume sites you should use an Emoji. An Emoji is a little icon or picture you place in your photo instead of you.

The same is not true for social networking sites like Twitter or Instagram where they are less business-like and casual environments. An Emoji is fine on Facebook or other casual websites and social sites. The business of job hunter and job searching is not that casual. You may get solicitations and job offers with an Emoji instead of your face, but I can guarantee you have missed getting contacted at some point in time. Be mature and you will be fine.

Using Great Images In Your Articles

Before I finish writing a LinkedIn article I almost always look for a cool, relatable image for my article to add to the top of the article when I publish it. It is critical to get people's attention to have great images as opposed to no image or images that are weak, visually out of focus or completely misguided like negative images that should never be put on LinkedIn. I personally swear by Unsplash.com, a great image website that allows the free personal use of images for the purpose of writing blog articles.

Additional Profile Media Content

One of the techniques top marketers use is to leave a PDF file beneath a job to allow potential hirers to watch a presentation originally from PowerPoint. This is a great way to introduce your design and marketing skills if that is your background! You can also upload other types of content to your profile under a job listing. Remember, using this content to promote you is what this is all about. Taking advantage of this opportunity in showing more content is what you need to do outmaneuver your competition.

#4 LinkedIn SEO Tagging

The world of SEO and getting found on Google often revolves around tagging. Tagging or Hash Tagging for

Twitter is another reference to adding keywords to an article or online post in a way to get found better. Most Hash Tagging requires putting a # in front of a keyword like #WebAnalytics.

For LinkedIn, the best way to get yourself found is to add job experiences which have all the relevant keywords in the job descriptions. Leaving out the actual description of what you did on the job is not good. These words are used for the internal LinkedIn search for YOU.

The next best way on LinkedIn to get tagged properly is to increase your Featured Skills and Endorsement. If you have been using LinkedIn for a while these skills may be added by people who have given you a recommendation on LinkedIn. Regardless of whether you added it or not, these skills are the tags needed to get your profile discovered, so don't take them for granted.

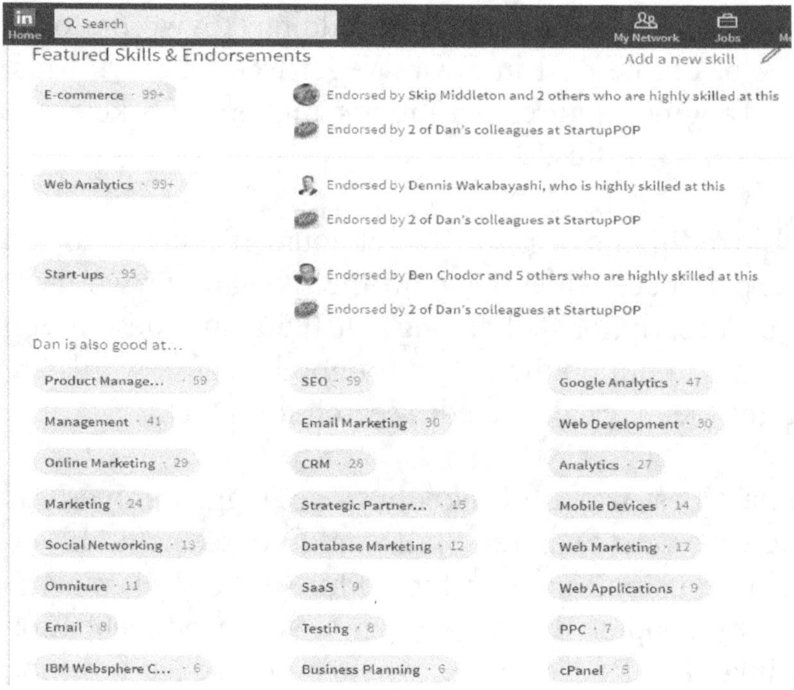

Notice you need to constantly work on improving your featured skills & endorsement area, keeping it up to date with your skillset.

The world of LinkedIn is a never ending situation for most of us. We need to be consistently working on our LinkedIn profile. The best way to keep relevant is writing original content on LinkedIn as articles as well as making posts and commenting on posts. If you have always felt this is something other people do, you may be questioning yourself. Remember, the more times your name shows up under searches or posts or comments, the more chances a potential employer will find you, read about you and contact you. So, if you have never written a LinkedIn blog article or posted, the time to start is now.

#5 *Increasing And Building Your LinkedIn Community*

One of the reasons you want to increase the number of connections you have on LinkedIn is when you publish on LinkedIn, the first group that will see your article summary with a picture is your connections. If you have less than 100 connections, then your articles may not get viewed very well. To get your articles viewed by thousands or tens of thousands you need to have LinkedIn Followers. How do you get these followers? Well, let's just say if you are not famous or well-known in your field you are pretty much out of luck to start off big. But there is hope for the rest of us non-Kardashians. The best thing for you to do is to write a few articles and get others to comment and to share your articles as well as share your articles outside of LinkedIn.

Social Sharing of LinkedIn Articles

I have had some success using Twitter in particular for sharing LinkedIn subject matter articles. In other words, very few other mediums other than Facebook have brought me article viewers. Once again Facebook viewers tended to be old friends and family and then other friends of friends and family. Old friends and family are not looking to hire you, so using Facebook won't work very well other than getting you a bunch of snide remarks from your family and friends. My Facebook followers, which are high school, college friends and relatives probably think I am nuts because I let my LinkedIn articles flow to Facebook. They see me doing business on Facebook and probably wonder what is wrong with me. I have said not to go there, but it is another place I can share! You just have to have no limit to what you will make your relatives put up with!

It is on Twitter that you probably need to sync up your personal brand image and communications if you are going to attract employers and headhunters and use the connections you have to build up your LinkedIn followers. Just like yourself, industry compatriots or people in the same industry, will want to connect with you because you never know, in the future they may be looking for a job and you may be looking to be hired.

7

<u>BLOGGING = LEADERSHIP</u>

Let's take a little tour of a blogging site I love to blog on called Medium.com.

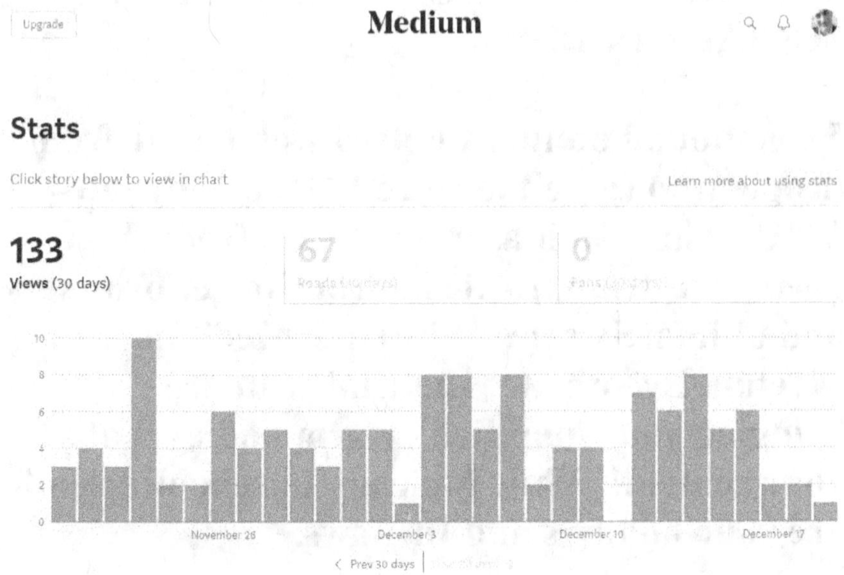

Notice how Medium shows you great stats about how many people are viewing your articles.

The best thing about Medium is the breadth and quality of blogging are really better than most blog sites. There are literally millions of independent blogs, as well as Blogger and WordPress.com where you can blog. The reason I love blogging on Medium, is they seem to be drawing in more traffic to my subject matter expertise which has been startups, web analytics, and the online dating industry. So in a sense, they seem to be a great place for visitors for all three of these subject matters. In fact, they may actually be specifically for these industries.

GO SEO YOURSELF TIP #9

UNDERSTAND WHICH WEBSITES ARE A MARKET AND WHICH ARE A PERSONAL SOCIAL CLUB!

To get found online you need web traffic from people who can either hire YOU or buy into YOU. Think of it as a retail storefront. You need pedestrian traffic in order to get browsers and ultimately sales. Sites like Medium, Meetup, Eventbrite, and LinkedIn are bringing you "qualified" warm bodies that see your content! While typically Facebook friends are your buddy's and In-Laws.

The real question is why blog at all?

Obviously, I like to blog because I have always been a writer and that is how I have lived my life for the past 40 years, writing on a daily basis. I have been writing consistently since I was ten years old and used to write in bound journals. I would guess I have written over 250 blog articles in the past 11 years. That includes what we refer to as both long form and short form blog articles. I really specialize in long form, which means I get to at least 3 full pages of writing each time. For me blogging and writing, in general, has been instinctual. It is in the blood. I started as a physical journal writer when I was 10 and I have pretty much written weekly and monthly and sometimes daily ever since. When blogging came along as a thing to do around 2006, I was the first person on the bandwagon.

There are so many other reasons to blog other than the fact that I like to write. The reason I blog has turned from "expressing" myself to how I educate people with knowledge and ultimately provide leadership.

Why you need to blog may be very different than why I need to blog. Some of us are trying to enhance our career and get a job. Some are trying to be self-help gurus. Good luck with that career. Some are trying to sell you something and every once in a while there is a blogger who is actually trying to help the world or save the world. Also, good luck with that! I like to write about many things I specifically have knowledge on like this book and using SEO to get hired! You need to figure out what you are an expert at and how you can communicate that through blogging.

Aha Moments

My blogs start as ideas and they develop into concepts and short outlines and eventually, a full point of view emerges on subjects that turn into a blog article. Many times my networking conversations evolve into discussing something important with a colleague. That's when I have an Aha moment. Usually, it comes from a conversation with one of my personal community members or my mentors.

Below is a list of articles I wrote over the past year. They focus on specific subjects that are of interest to me personally, but they also try to invite the reader in and hopefully they follow you for the next blog article when you   write   one.

2017

That's Not A Fact, It's An Opinion 7 min read · View story · Referrers	5 +2	2	40%
Will DIY YouTube Kill The Service Man? 5 min read · View story · Referrers	4	2	50%
The Startup Sell Test 6 min read · View story · Referrers	7 +1	3	43%
Why You Should Never Hire An Ex-Startup Person 6 min read · View story · Referrers	42	17	40%
The End Of The Gig Economy 5 min read · View story · Referrers	47	31	66%
Do You Need Intelligent Email? 3 min read · View story · Referrers	28	16	57%
Why The Pen Is Mightier Than The Sword When It Co... 5 min read · View story · Referrers	12 +20	4	33%
Google Analytics now Includes Sitelinks! 3 min read · View story · Referrers	8 +1	3	38%
Is It Time To Buy Gold Commodity Backed Bitcoin? 5 min read · View story · Referrers	133	63	47%
How To Interpret Twitter Analytics 6 min read · View story · Referrers	39	13	33%

These are recent articles I have published on Medium.

The first couple of books I wrote and self-published were a bunch of web blog articles I originally wrote and then weaved the blog articles together into a book. This book was actually not exactly created that way. Most of the content in this book is fresh and new and not free to read online somewhere in one of my blog articles, though I will publish some of the excerpts from this book in my blogs.

Whether I was a subject expert before I blogged about the subject is not important. Writing about a subject can make you an expert. Having an opinion and describing and teaching through writing or trying to accomplish something for the good of society through writing, that's what we call leadership in my book.

Leadership is a simple-to-understand concept. Blogging is one way to be a leader with just writing. It's not the writing that is the leadership. It's the point of having an opinion and explaining things and trying to change and improve things. Just the act of writing about anything means you are leading and becoming an authority on that subject.

What is the positive impact of blogging for YOU personally?

There is a major positive impact for you to write blogs and most are SEO related. The first and most important is personal satisfaction. Every time I finish a blog and publish, I know that I have created something unique and different that nobody can take away from me. It is my own writing.

Then there are the technical SEO benefits of blogging. This is a very important concept you need to understand in this book. Obviously writing about a subject matter makes you an authority as well as the keywords and content. That authority is recognized by Google's search engine as important and it results in higher ranked content. Eventually it will be more important for the job site internal search engines. Being an authority through blogging is your way of leading in your industry.

One the most important and not really looked at part of the SEO of blogging is small information like date and time of the article and other small details. While it may not sound important, the details are critical for SEO. Blog articles are looked at by the search engines as recent and newsworthy content. That makes them show up higher.

The article title tag and what we call H1, H2, H3 and H4 titles and other similar HTML tags are highly regarded by Google as important content. You don't need to know what they are, but you do need to know they exist and as you blog they get generated for Google to know about the content. If you blog with WordPress or on LinkedIn, these HTML tags get built for you automatically. They can get your content to show up higher in Google.

Categorization and tagging are critical parts of blogging. They can be used to boost SEO content and further index the blog article. This means the more categories and tags you can assign an article the better for SEO purposes.

Most blog creation tools like WordPress automatically create a page per category and page per tag. I have written a blog article on WordPress with 10 categories and 25 separate tags. The end result is 36 pages of content to Google. So don't underestimate the value of blogging and getting found through blogging.

LinkedIn does not have great categorization and tagging. They limit you to 3 tags. That's pretty lame in SEO terms. The same is true of Medium. So for the ones which allow unlimited tagging, like WordPress, it is a major advantage. For LinkedIn articles, you have to rely on the content mostly getting indexed nicely on Google in addition to the article Title and Excerpt. That's why LinkedIn articles sometimes don't get indexed on Google as well as my personal website, which is WordPress.

If you have a WordPress website, the blog attached to it can be quite important. Don't underestimate the value of this blog to SEO. You should have your own website and it should be WordPress based!

Similar to articles on LinkedIn, blog articles are important to be created on a regular basis for consistency. Also, articles with inbound and outbound links increase the value on Google.

What I would recommend is start monthly and write an article on a subject you want to communicate about which can increase your authority within your industry. Don't feel embarrassed, overwhelmed or that this activity is stupid. You have to work your way through it and get it done and done over again. You may want to sit on an article and rewrite it several times. I have some drafts I am sitting on a year later I have not published for various reasons like I have not had the time for that article or I just don't like the tone or who will be reading it may get upset with me. ☺

The Pitch

I like to refer to <u>The Pitch</u> at the end of a blog article. If you were to write an article and get somebody's attention, I think it is important to pitch them on something at the end. In my case, I have used articles to get people to attend local events. And I have also used the articles to convince people to join my mailing list. In some cases, I have used the end of the article to push a product or service. Sometimes I just don't ask people to do anything at all. Still you are really asking them to Follow you and connect with you, so in the end, you are really asking them to do this even if you don't ask! After I complete this book and publish it as an eBook, I will ask everyone who reads an article about the subject matter to go and either share a copy or buy a copy.

8

<u>ALL SUCCESSFUL PEOPLE WRITE A BOOK!</u>

Every once in a while I run into a person who says "I want to write and publish a book but I don't know how". My answer is always the same, "It is easy to self-publish a book, but hard to write one".

For SEO authority I am going to get into the weeds on why YOU need to write a book and how that will impact how you are viewed online overall and how it can impact your job search. Writing a book contributes tremendously to your SEO, how you are perceived and can really impact starting a new career and getting a gig.

But how can writing a book have an impact on your personal SEO?

Remember there is an authority you gain technically by having a book listed on Amazon, but there is some level of prestige associated with book writing. Trust me it is not about making money with books per se. In the non-fiction world of book publishing, guys who publish a yearly book like me are a dime a dozen. We turn out collectively thousands of non-fiction books every month that very few will read. In fact, that is why writing a book for the purpose of self-publishing is really not about making money selling the book. It is more about the biz it brings, the SEO value and authority you get from creating a book.

I feel in publishing a book, there is so much more to gain than just selling copies. As one of my mentors said sarcastically to people who made fun of me writing a book, *"Have you written a book?"* Their answer was *"No!"* So it is a bit of a moniker of personal success and positions you at a higher level online. You are a published author!

See how do these books get you SEO juice on Google. Let's first let's start with a search combining my name and Amazon on Google

The Google search results will show up when people look for you. Remember, after you have become a job candidate they will research you online. They will look for you on LinkedIn, but before the employer searches LinkedIn, they typically search Google. Having these results show up when they search Google solidifies your authority on the subject.

If you take a look at my book listings on Amazon, notice the fact that the name of the author shows up on each book page. There is a link to the author page on every Amazon page. The number of people about to purchase a book that click on an author page is significant. And the first couple pages of a book, for the Kindle version, get indexed by Google as well.

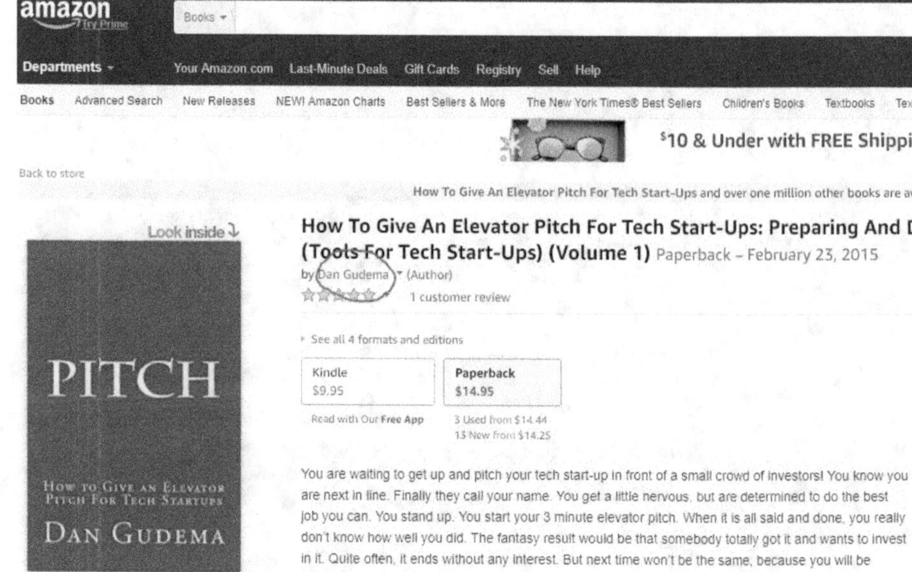

Next, let's take a look at one of my book pages on Amazon. That red circle is a link to my author page. Click on any author to view their author page on Amazon. Or if you want to review my author page, click on mine!

Notice on my author page all the content in my bio and how it has SEO built into it. Notice that the same page shows my blog posts from Twitter. That's because Amazon has allowed me to integrate Twitter with my Amazon bio page. How would you know that? Well, I am telling you that's how it works and why it is important to do all these things in concert with one another.

The content in my bio is well indexed on Google. In fact, everything in this Amazon bio page is well indexed. That is why you need to have a book or books listed on Amazon. The authority level of Amazon itself propels this content be shown higher up on Google. If you put your keywords and search terms that are yours into that bio, you can master this part of the web for SEO.

But How Difficult Is It To Publish A Book?

A website years ago was acquired by Amazon called CreateSpace at CreateSpace.com. I have used CreateSpace to create all my books and have spent little to nothing on the making of my books. CreateSpace is free to use. Amazon (which is the CreateSpace parent) only gets paid when we publish and sell books as a commission. It is a high commission, but I have put up no dollars up front.

My books have been sold all around the world and I have published a ton of copies. Most of these copies were printed and sold by me directly. In fact, Amazon only publishes my book when I want a copy. This is the new world of on-demand publishing.

For online publishing, there are a variety of options. Obviously publishing through Kindle is the most likely one you will choose as well. The thing you need to understand about Kindle and Amazon Store together is the first couple of pages are often shown to customers. Those first couple of pages are from the Kindle part of publishing. So, if you are going to use CreateSpace.com and create a printed book, you should also create a Kindle version or eBook version.

Just like CreateSpace, Kindle is free to use and easy to do. I have also used Gumroad.com because it charges a much lower commission than Amazon. Use Gumroad if you are self-publishing and you are only going to sell direct yourself. If you know who is going to buy then Amazon is a waste of money. This is for those who really don't care about Amazon sales. If you are the seller as well and it is an online only deal, then shouldn't you make more per ebook?

What Should You Write About?

When writing a book, the book should be something you are knowledgeable about or want to be knowledgeable about. But overall you will be an expert on that subject once you finish it.

How I started recent books is by first writing a couple blog articles that would be the foundation of the book. After you find some success in blogging about the subject, then it may be time to write your book.

What you need consider in writing a book is the end result. It is a different goal per person. I use writing as a way to get authority and notoriety and SEO juice from being listed as an author. Then there are a ton of additional opportunities to get listed as a speaker or doing book openings. And being an expert in a subject matter is part of what I call creating *authority*. Being an author is part of that equation.

9

VIDEO, AUDIO, IMAGES AND STREAMING

Just think about the fact that every picture you post, every video and even audio you publish online gets you even more authority and even better Google search results. Google will move these media files, images, and videos higher up on Google. They have separate indexes for these media. There is even a search for photos.

GO SEO YOURSELF TIP #10

USE RICH SNIPPETS TO GET SEEN ON GOOGLE!

Rich Snippets are little pieces of content and HTML code on a website that lets Google know what to show within your Google search

results. It's why your listing on Google will look a little different, typically nicer with dates, times, locations and other little tidbits in the how the results show up naturally. Just happens that if you combine images, video and rich snippets on a web page you can show up on Google in a nice looking.

Below is an example of Rich Snippets at work. Notice how the content shows up formatted differently by Google. These visual cues help people out by pushing content into Google and give people a reason to click compared with ordinary listings. The listings at the top, if you are lucky enough to get Youtube to profile you, allow you to have your content bigger, and in a nicer format.

Uploads from Daniel Gudema - YouTube
www.youtube.com/playlist?list=UUJ5uhkWhBWK76Chu4mfrXKQ ▾
by **Daniel Gudema**. 11:39. Play next; Play now. StartupPOP Pitch Jan 25, 2017. by **Daniel Gudema**. 1:27. Play next; Play now. Idate 2017 Big Data, Web Analytics, Business Intelligence. by **Daniel Gudema**. 1:05. Play next; Play now. Max is human techno sound effect, a MLG YTP **YouTube** Poop. by **Daniel Gudema**. 0:29.

StartupPOP Boca Raton 04-26-17 - Dan Gudema Intro ... - YouTube
https://www.youtube.com/watch?v=7_ccQKPz2dM
Apr 28, 2017 - Uploaded by StartupPOP Tech Startup Pitch Events
This video is **Dan Gudema's** intro at a presentation in a series which covers a Startup Pitch Event in South ...

Will YouTube DIY Kill The Service Man? | Dan Gudema | Pulse ...
https://www.linkedin.com/pulse/youtube-diy-kill-radio-repairman-dan-gudema ▾
Oct 10, 2017 - Have you ever had your refrigerator ice maker break? Have you ever had your washing machine pump stop pumping? Have you had your dryer door hinge break? Have you had your toilet just start flushing over and over? Have you had the cord snap on an XBox 360? Have you cracked the back of your ...

Notice how the video image gets listed on Google search results showing the video time and the first image.

This image below is a good example of how Rich Snippets can be used to make the Google search results much more interactive, passes content to Google results and easier to understand. Every once in a while Google will show your results in a nicely formatted way that is different than other results if your results are the authority on the subject. It determines this authority by choosing the first listing in the search results!

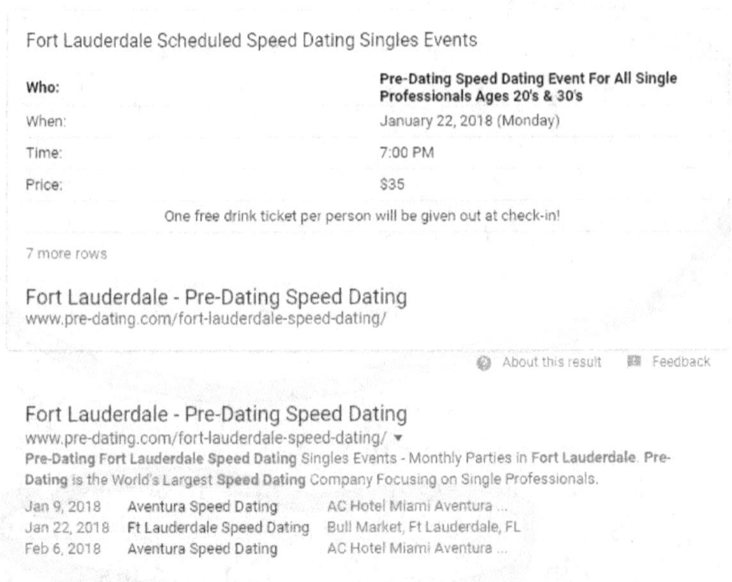

A few years ago I began to recognize the power of images and video on SEO.

More specifically I noticed that Youtube listings and images were being indexed by Google differently and given preference.

Also, I believe video will for now and into the future be

the best way to promote yourself and message online. It's pretty obvious. I am comparing a flat world of text that we live in today in Google searches with a TV like 3D world of video.

People are less likely to be reading this book than watching a video. My belief and knowledge of video started to increase when my children started to follow Youtube superstars. These are ordinary people who got themselves so well situated on Youtube, where some of these Youtube superstars get millions of viewers per video. A lot of the views are for gamers, who watch other people's gaming videos. My sons have been addicted to this for years.

So how can video impact your job search?

I first tried video when I was running the Meetups and community events I created out of Boca Raton, Florida. What I would do is create a video for some of the events to talk about the startup pitch events I run and what to expect during the event. I would post the video on Youtube specifically. Why is video and Youtube in particular so important for SEO? The results of creating Youtube videos is they show up higher in searches. That's because Youtube is owned by Google and tightly integrated with Google.

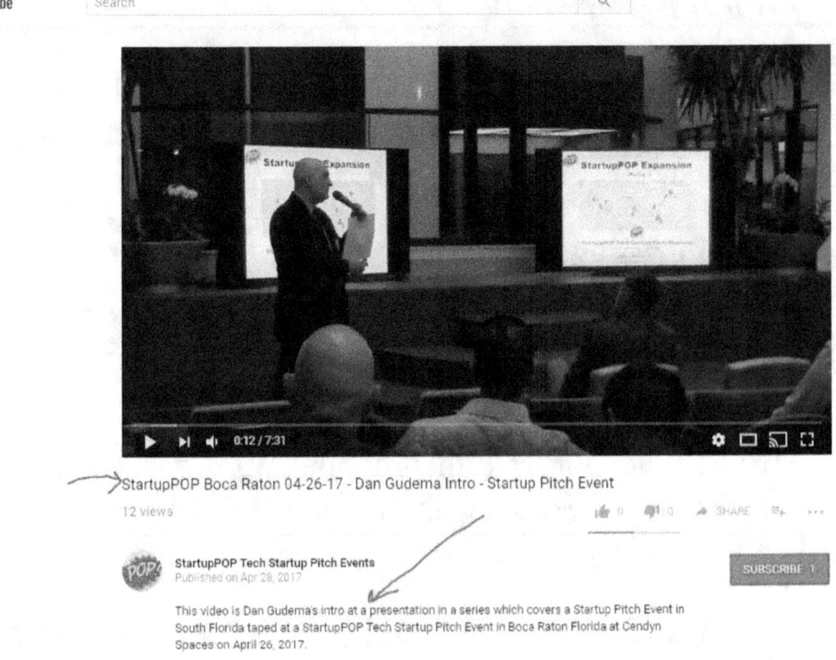

StartupPOP Boca Raton 04-26-17 - Dan Gudema Intro - Startup Pitch Event

12 views

StartupPOP Tech Startup Pitch Events
Published on Apr 28, 2017

This video is Dan Gudema's intro at a presentation in a series which covers a Startup Pitch Event in South Florida taped at a StartupPOP Tech Startup Pitch Event in Boca Raton Florida at Cendyn Spaces on April 26, 2017.

SHOW MORE

Notice how on this Youtube page the Title has SEO keywords and the content had SEO keywords.

It's important to really make sure if you do a video on Youtube to make sure it has nice SEO content that matches your personal branding keywords. In my case, if I were to record and post a video I would want to use either "web analytics", "WordPress" or "e-commerce" in my Youtube text content area. Every item on Youtube including the Title content and the main content are important to your SEO authority.

What is Periscope?

Periscope is a free smartphone App that allows you to live stream video of anything like places and people to audiences all around the world.

When Periscope first came out as a free app, I was totally obsessed watching Periscope streaming videos from all around the world. Eventually, I started to live stream my pitch events.

If you have not tried this mobile app based system or its competitor Meerkat, it is time to catch up with the world of technology.

I blogged about how Periscope got me a bunch of followers and helped promote my brand. A few people asked me how to use Periscope and though I could not give them a specific answer other than you can use it to promote yourself or whatever you are doing, I can show you the results of the periscopes of my pitch events.

First, you need to understand that Periscope is part of Twitter. So when you start live streaming, your Twitter account tells people you are live and online. The second part of this is the entire video and stream, which can be excellent quality can be stored and saved as a video file that goes on Youtube and can be replayed by Periscope users for days following the event. For 24 hours you can download.

Later on, Periscope and several other sites index your Periscope title and information and list these short videos on Google. So you are getting more and more backlinks this way. So if you are going to Periscope, remember to name your titles very carefully with your keywords. Your Periscope video may be around for years as SEO content.

GO SEO YOURSELF TIP #11

INCREASING YOUR BACKLINKS INCREASES YOUR SEO AUTHORITY!

Backlinks are another way of describing websites with a link to your website. By increasing the number of inbound URL web links to your website, you increase your authority which means Google will list you higher. That's another way you get higher in the Google rankings. So, the big question is how to increase backlinks?

10

PRESS, TWITTER & HARO

Around the time I started to create startup pitch events in Boca Raton, Florida to promote my brand and build up an online and offline community I began to invest my time in trying a variety of social media to promote myself. What I was looking for was a way to promote the startup pitch events, and the events were a bigger way to promote myself and my services.

Just to let you know the real reason I started those events was to find outsourced web development projects, and that is how I got paid at the time. I used the events initially to draw in large crowds interested in startups, technology, and venture capital. A byproduct of this event and community building was finding startup software development projects. I was looking for projects I could work on as a consultant and send to a team in Ukraine to do the work. That actually worked out until the Ukrainian software company owner and I had a falling out. After that happened and I was no longer taking on startup projects, I realized that the events and the community building itself were good for me and my career.

A lot of people will do the action of getting the press to draw traffic and to push people through their marketing funnel.

GO SEO YOURSELF TIP #12

USE A MARKETING FUNNEL TO GET PEOPLE TO YOUR GOAL.

A marketing funnel is the journey you create for your customers from the first moment they read about you to the point where they convert in some way. Most conversions are a buy, but a follow could be the end result. If you are looking for a job, your marketing funnel is about getting employers and headhunters to notice you and convert by contacting you! You need to recognize every step of the marketing funnel and you should try to understand how many people you are starting with and how

many are ending up contacting you. There are stats on every job site telling you how many views your resume received in searches.

When it comes to SEO, most people getting press know they want to get people to take a specific action, called a goal, like getting people to fill out a form or signup. The goal of online press is traffic and completions. For social media, the goal may be a little different, like getting more links to your primary pages and website. These URLS embedded in social media are called these backlinks.

Backlinks

We used to call backlinks referring URLs. Reciprocal backlinks are great also great for SEO. That's when you both site have links to each other. Basically, the name of the game is getting your site, your name, and links mentioned on third-party sites with authority. A mention means there is a link back to your site. And this includes any newspaper, magazine, blog or anyplace online where you can get a mention with your keywords.

What I discovered out about promoting my brand and ultimately my career was, for at least tech startup related events, that Twitter in my case was right behind Meetup and Eventbrite as a top priority. It was at the top of the social media for my startup target market. Startups were very drawn to Twitter and it served that market well. I was able to get several thousand followers. It's funny, because to some Twitter experts, a couple thousand is not a lot. But I can tell you that my Twitter following was not like other people's Twitter following. And often people buy Twitter followers. I don't recommend that.

Eventually, I took some time to look at the analytics that Twitter provides and lo and behold among the 2,000 followers that @dgudema had on Twitter, the average household income was over $200,000. That's because Twitter followers of hashtag #startup were Venture Capital Fund Managers and ex-successful tech startups in Silicon Valley. They began following me in large numbers.

That brings me to the next thing to know about social media. While other tools like Facebook and Meetup can be more centered around where you are located, you can't really control the location basis of your Twitter following, leaving out people from other cities and countries. That's why I ended up with thousands of followers from around the world, which is great for SEO purposes and getting found, but not great for getting me a job locally.

While you can control and manage a group in your physical area on Meetup, where Meetup goes out and promotes your local events, Twitter goes everywhere. So, the issue here is only about 20% of my followers were local to South Florida. This is a particularly important consideration in how you want your SEO to work. There is a whole book we could write on just getting your SEO right for the physical location that we refer to as "local". Just consider that if you are looking for a job locally, you need to be discovered by employers locally, not around the country. In my job searches, I found it better to be looking around the country for work. It was part of my strategy.   I felt that I was willing to go anywhere (maybe) and I was also looking for remote work I could bring back to Florida. In the end, I felt looking everywhere helps to find a job locally for me.

GO SEO YOURSELF TIP #13

LOCATION-BASED MARKETING IS AN IMPORTANT SEO TECHNIQUE

Google highly values location data, so your city, your state, your zip code, even your physical address or the venue and address of events are important tags you need to make sure are on as many pieces of content you write and create online. The impact for people with geo-coded smartphone who search the Internet will be that your local content is given a bump up in the search results.

On Twitter, I originally thought it was not helping me getting followers from cities that I was not like San Francisco for running startup pitch events.   That was until we started to expand the startup events to other cities, like New York City, where it has been quite successful.

What I discovered is the larger the Twitter following, the greater chance of not just getting attendees to my events, but I would often get people who would retweet about my events even if they were in Timbuktu. All your retweeters and followers are now your army or your community on Twitter. Just be aware of what they can and cannot do for you. Also, remember the golden rule, do unto others as they would do for you. Whenever anyone asked me to promote their event, their startup, their job search, I typically helped them, no charge.

This is an important consideration. Twitter tweets get indexed by Google. This is really important. So take a look at how these tweets have been nicely indexed on Google:

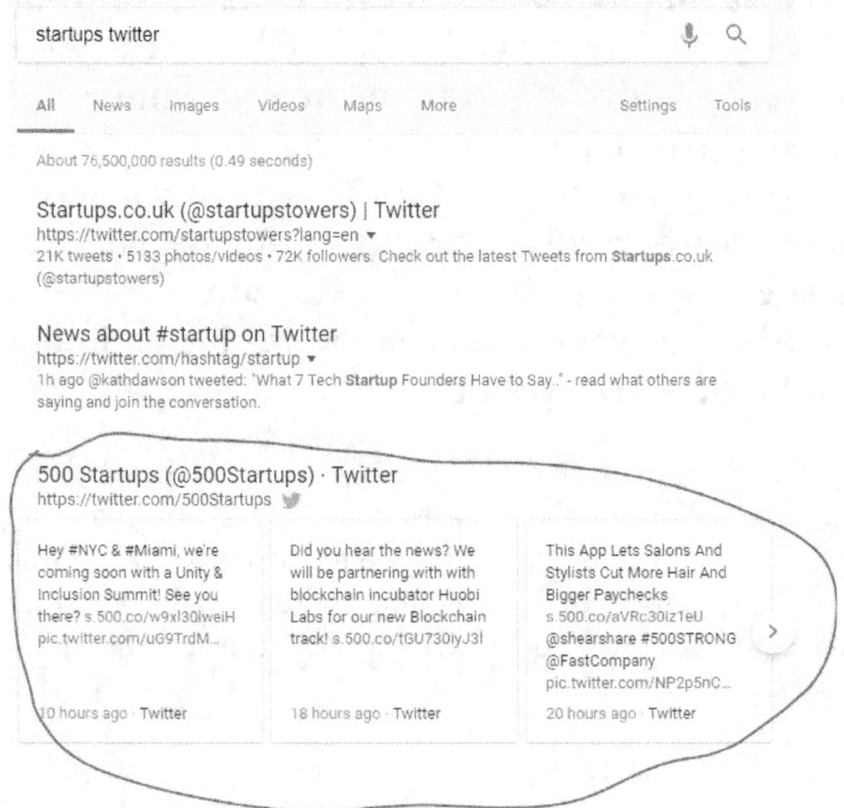

HARO – Help A Reporter Out

A couple years ago my wife mentioned to me HARO – Help A Reporter Out, https://www.helpareporter.com/, (as a way to get my events and startup community promoted. Basically, HARO has two functions. One is to be the journalist and ask questions. That costs money. The other one is to be the one who answers the questions for journalists. That one is free.

But why would you want to answer questions in HARO? The answer is backlinks or mentions on top websites like news sites. And this type of link is Google gold when it comes to SEO. It may be a good thing for your reputation as well. HARO allowed me to get a mention of my startup community on both Inc. Magazine and in Forbes. More importantly, I was personally mentioned in a quote. That means I can actually say I was mentioned in magazines.

The technical reason why you want to get a mention online is the backlinks are A+. That means you can't get anything better than a mention from the Wall Street Journal or New York Times for instance. I came so close at one point to not just being mentioned in the Harvard Business Review, where they were going to do an article profiling me with my story. That would have been a personal dream of mine and great for SEO, but I ended up getting edited out of the article at the last minute.

What is the downside of working with HARO? It's not so much a downside, but you need to answer their questions and not dictate what you want to say. That means this is about the link and maybe your authority but not about your message. It is about what story they are looking to write. It has to be answered on the terms of the journalist. They have already decided on the article and typically your interview or comments are just minor content they need as testimony or real live person add-on content. So sometimes to get yourself mentioned, you need to lower the bar a bit. As my wife put it, do you have no shame in what you will talk about? They have a lot of subjects on there that are racy. Most are current subjects about lifestyles, politics and finance and health. If it is a popular subject in the news, they are writing about it. If you are willing to go out on a limb and answer these questions, I say go for it! I have had major success using it.

How Do You Work With HARO?

Let's say you want to go for it and work with HARO. First, you need to find HARO's website and sign up. Once you have registered officially, you need to read the HARO requests which arrive by email every day. Choose a question and send in your response from the exact email address you registered with and make sure the subject is the question ID. Get any of those items wrong and it will reject you immediately.

HARO is relatively easy to work with once you get it set up. That means you virtually never have to log in again if you are set up. You just read the emails and respond to the email for everything. That's a great way to work with a system.

11

INSTAGRAM AND PINTEREST VISUALIZATION

If you are a web designer, in the fashion business as your career or any career where something visual needs to be expressed in your line of business, then the focus of the social media for building SEO and authority should be on Instagram and Pinterest, and not necessarily Twitter or Facebook. For instance, if you are in the Yacht business and there are vessels you need to show, then you are in a visually optimized online profession. Are you a chef, model, painter, web designer, brand manager, clothes designer or carpenter? Instagram and Pinterest make total sense for professions where everything visual shows what you do. For instance, the accounting profession has little to know visualizations compared with someone who is a chef or works with clothing.

GO SEO YOURSELF TIP #14

ONLY FOCUS ON SOCIAL MEDIA THAT MAKES SENSE FOR YOU

Everyone has a Facebook, Twitter and Instagram icon on every home page. But the truth is that certain social media help you and certain social media are a waste of time depending on the industry you are in. And there are a ton of choices to focus on. Just happens my focus was on startups, so Instagram and Pinterest made very little sense for me personally. Any significant time I would have put into these social media would have been wasted!

If you are in a business that needs visualization, then collecting and displaying images is more important in your industry than others. Examples are chefs, fashionistas, realtors, health and beauty. You need to take advantage of this visualization to increase your chances of being found online by being one of the thousands who create Pinterest pages or become heavy users of Instagram, which is a visualization-based social media channel.

My first real experience with one of these visual industries is when I went to work as an e-commerce consultant for a sportswear company. We were making high-end shorts and tees for people who lifted, ran and worked out. Their entire social media focused on Instagram. The whole sportswear industry was focused on Instagram. They also had some Pinterest images that were getting thousands of clicks.

You have to figure out what everybody else is doing within your industry. Once you figure this out, you can create your Pinterest pages or your Instagram posts and focus in on this area.

Google Images & Google Photos & Google+

There are a hundred potential online tools you may consider using to promote yourself. Some are created by the largest companies on the web that are worth pursuing and taking time to master. When it comes to getting your visual message out about yourself, I have found some small pockets of value with certain services. For instance, using Google to promote additional images, you will get those images indexed and sometimes it is easier to get photos indexed than content, especially when there is a lack of photos.

Google+ is Google's social network. There has been some anecdotal evidence it may not be around much longer, but still, it is a great place to upload images that are job search and career-related. I have participated in web analytics Google+ groups where a community works together to solve specific web analytics questions and issues concerning Google Analytics. When using this particular social network you have to always understand that the content, especially images, when made public, will flow to the search engines. One of the things I have focused on is occasionally discussing web analytic subjects and solutions on Google+, because like everywhere else you need to be online for SEO. Google+, in particular, could be the place where a head-hunter or employer begins their search for a professional.

In fact, head-Hunters are pretty much running out of places to look for candidates. That is why you need to be on a social network like Google+. Not sure how active you need to be, but being active means contributing, commenting on a regular basis. It all adds up that you are the authority on that subject and by Google's standards SEO authority means you show up at the top of the search engine listings.

12

GOOGLE SEO CIRCLES OF INFLUENCE

This chapter is about how Google SEO really works. It is also my theory on how it works, because honestly nobody knows exactly how it works other than Google.

For the uninitiated, when people search Google the question is how high up will your results appear? On what page will they appear? Will it be on page 1? That's a simple question to ask? Right?

I wish it was simple...because it is not a simple question!

Notice on this Google results listing that my listing shows up on page one and entices the employer to contact me!

A couple years ago I worked as a Web Analytics & Business Intelligence/SQL consultant for a drug rehab organization that was throwing thousands of dollars each month into search engine optimization, trying to get found on Google. They had a good reason. Just one conversion to their services was worth thousands of dollars.

An exec asked me a simple question. What is their website "page rank" in terms of showing up on Google? He wanted to know where they should up when people searched for "drug rehab".

As I would quickly find out, and as many of you in the online marketing and the web analytics business already know, Google Page Rank is long dead, long ago.

This exec wanted to know their website's Page Rank! A 10-second search of Google came back with the answer that Page Rank is gone long ago. There is no tool out there to get the old Page Rank. Page Rank used to be a number assigned to the value of each web page.

Anyone who claims to get page rank for you is just making something up. The only thing they can use today is "Average Page Rank". And the concept of page rank is much more complicated than that. Every single person on Google is getting personalized search results! We all see something different when we do a Google search! Explain that to the higher-ups!

So I began a journey as a tech guy into how Google seems to work (my theory) and ultimately, a few months later I finally had an answer to how to figure out page rank or page position as they now call it. You can get some "Search Term Page Positioning" approximations for FREE if you just hack around and make a few clicks here and there.

I ended up coming up with a theory as to how Google currently ranks all web pages. And based on this, how YOU should consider managing your personal career SEO and all the other possible social media and other stuff involved with getting ranked nicely "per person" on Google.

On an aside, what is my SEO cred?

Go to Google and type in "Seattle Speed Dating" or "Fort Lauderdale Speed Dating" or a 100 other cities with the words "speed dating". Our company, Pre-Dating.com's website is either #1 or first page naturally in 100s of searches. So, I guess I know something.

Circles of Influence: My SEO Theory

I am not saying this is exactly how it all works because it almost seems so complicated that even Google employees themselves probably don't know every variable at this point in determining what gets ranked higher for what reason. But let's just say that there are Circles of Influence. These are the critical "relatively new" influence factors. And it has and will change in the future. There is a long list of traditional and real old circle of influence factors you need to have in place like Page Title, Meta Descriptions, and Keyword Density <H1> tags. That is old school stuff that needs to be done. I am talking the new high influencing variables. See at the bottom of this graphic I threw together that says old school!

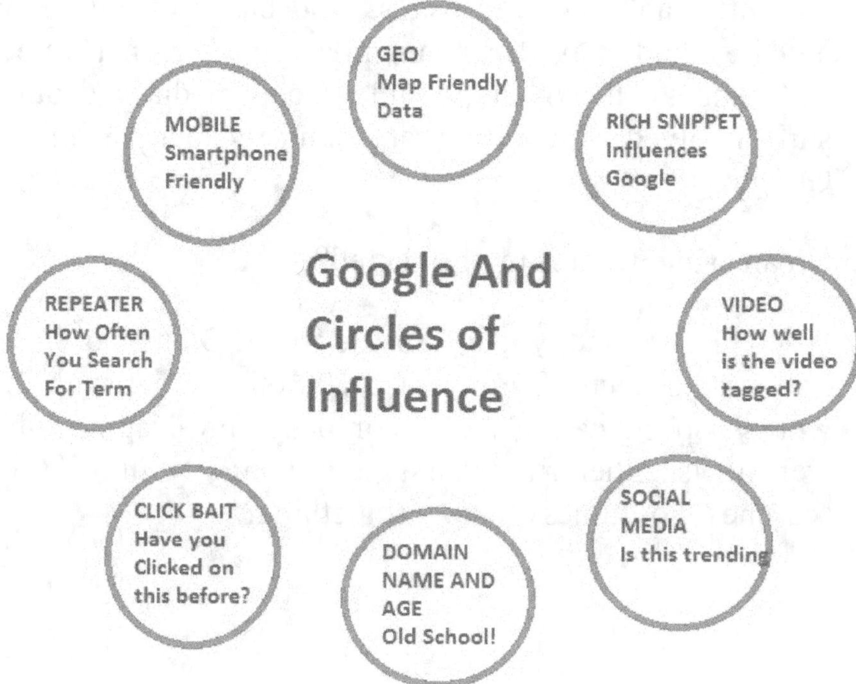

What are Circles of Influence and how does that work?

In my head, I imagine a bunch of circles per each Google Search. Each circle is a factor related to your search.

So what is the Influence of each of these Circles of Influence?

Well, this is the secret sauce Google won't let us know. Let's just say that each person search gets different results. There is a different search per person so it is truly unknown! Try explaining that to some executives.

Using AI (Artificial Intelligence) as we surf, it is going to depend on whether we are on mobile, our physical geo proximity, how often we search, repeat searches, how often we buy, what we buy and a dozen other top factors. So when an exec wants to know the exact Page Rank or position, the proper word to use is Average Page Position or AVP (per keyword). Remember not to use the term Average Page Position without the word keyword, because otherwise, it is pretty much ridiculous. And where does that AVP come from? Well, you can now get it through the Google Analytics "Search Console". See below, my real data for a few days on Pre-Dating.com. The only thing you can use it for is to tell me you want to buy our company. And we are for sale of course!

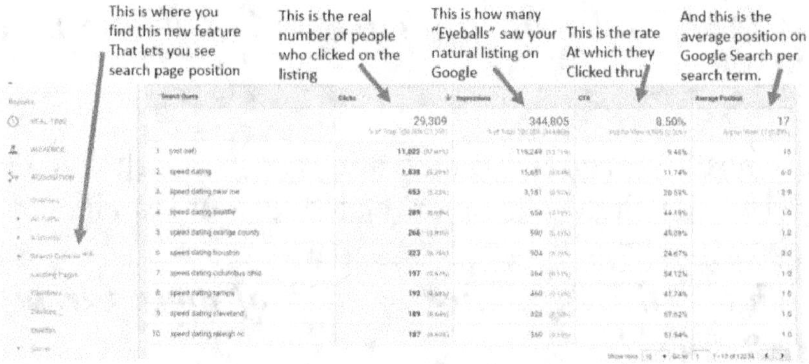

This is where you find this new feature That lets you see search page position

This is the real number of people who clicked on the listing

This is how many "Eyeballs" saw your natural listing on Google

This is the rate At which they Clicked thru

And this is the average position on Google Search per search term.

Search Query	Clicks	Impressions	CTR	Average Position
	29,309	344,805	8.50%	17
1. (not set)	11,022	116,249	9.46%	15
2. speed dating	1,838	15,681	11.74%	6.0
3. speed dating near me	653	3,161	20.53%	3.9
4. speed dating seattle	289	654	44.19%	1.0
5. speed dating orange county	266	590	45.09%	1.2
6. speed dating houston	223	904	24.67%	3.0
7. speed dating columbus ohio	197	364	54.12%	1.0
8. speed dating tampa	192	460	41.74%	1.0
9. speed dating cleveland	189	328	57.62%	1.0
10. speed dating raleigh nc	187	360	51.54%	1.0

Actually, it is very specifically in Google Analytics under Web Analytics/Acquisition/Search Console and then you have to click on "Queries". For SEO purposes this has now become the most important area of Google Analytics in my mind. And not sure how long this has been around because this data I believe was available in Google Search Console/Web Master Tools for a while, but not exactly as useful as this is, where it is now positioned!

Now, how to really tell what the Heck is Going On?

Well, in addition to all these tools, I always turn to Anonymous Browsing to get a sense of what the real world is seeing on Google. I use Anonymouse.org. It lets me surf as a guy in northern California unencumbered by the stigma of the circles of influence like Mobile, Geo, Repeat, etc. What I often find by searching through Anonymous Browsing is a completely different view than what I see. Because we are often working on websites where what we see can be completely not the true picture!

Finally, what is my current rank of importance in influence?

Once again, totally MY OPINION on this. And I could be wrong because this is totally intuitive. Please consider this in your career SEO blogging, posting, creating profiles of content on resume sites! What I am trying to say is use these types of contents to get higher up in search results!

GEO - I just feel that having any city, zip code, address, state, country or other geographical markers in a web page will help influence things the most today. Most websites don't have the ability to use this because they are not Geo or location based on multiple locations. But if you have it, it could be critical.

MOBILE FRIENDLY - Like other developers I am looking at AMP, a new set of HTML/CSS by Google that makes your site even more mobile friendly. If your site is mobile friendly it will influence how high it shows.

RICH SNIPPETS - These take many forms today with about 4 methods. They are little codes on your website telling Google how to display and integrate the data in Google Searches. If you go to Schema.org you can learn more and if you use WordPress it is as simple as a plugin.

VIDEO - I am partial to video in that I believe Google is giving some higher influence on Video these days. Having it on your website and optimizing text around it through Youtube could be important.

I could go into a much more in-depth list of what comes next. Hopefully, this will give you a sense of what I mean by SEO!

13

<u>ALWAYS BE MEETING</u>

I added a couple of bonus chapters to this book to enhance your job search and really take advantage of the SEO you have so nicely built for yourself. This chapter will be straightforward about networking with people. It is not what you know but who you know. I believe that you should always interact with any reputable person who makes contact with you.

In fact, my wife has always wondered why I am going to lunch, dinner, and breakfast constantly meeting with people. It is not a coincidence that I have used the Internet to make all these contacts. Even in the case of the Meetups, I run and the people who want to interact with me from these Meetups, that I used the Internet to draw them in the Meetups. You have to determine what makes sense when you have found a new potential contact for a job or contract.

Is this person worth your time and energy?

The real question should be "How do you know in advance that this new contact is a waste of time?" You really don't. You don't know where you will find the next job or deal.

It takes a lot of time and energy to talk, chat, and meet and continually network. I have had to make sure that I am not just meeting for the sake of meeting. There are reasons I do all these lunches, coffees and meetings. You have to continually be out there working your networking contacts for the near future when you will need this community you have built to either find a job, solve a problem or other favors you need.

The last two jobs I had I was called by the employer themselves. The job right before these jobs I was brought in by a good friend and business associate. That is still the main way people find work. They find work through their network. So networking is the reason I go out and meet with people. You need a community, your own personal community you manage and communicate with in order to have a network. It's not like a friend of a friend of a friend will hook you up with a job interview. You need to make all contacts directly a primary contact if possible. That's why you need to make that connection and keep it handy. The only reason LinkedIn is the best way to connect is the connection will be permanent and you are digitally connected. Before LinkedIn, we had to keep a stack of business cards on our desk. I still do. And then we would have to enter those email addresses into a CRM or at least Gmail, which is essentially a CRM.

We are in a world where human contact has become rarer and rarer in the search for a job. I have personally met up with at least 10 local headhunters in the past year or 2. I want to keep them handy in case I need them. When I am in a job search, of course, I would like to know I can quickly contact them.

One of the most important aspects of meeting up with people is finding common ground, asking great questions and showing a general interest in people. Why do I have to mention this? Well, for one I am not always the best at being the one who asks the questions. I will admit I like to talk a lot. For people like me, possibly ADD, we need to have memorized ways of asking people questions. One is to get to know them well; the other is to make sure we sound empathetic, even if we are not. You need to be seen as a person they want to help out. But before they can help you, I always say to people "What can I do for you?"

Let's say somebody has asked you to meet with them and network for the first time. You never know when you will either need to look up this new contact, use this contact to get information or even have them land a job for you. You need to get out of the house and meet with people, especially if you work at home. Human contact is critical to future success for us in many ways, so don't under-value interactions you may have!

Mentoring = Learning

A few years ago I befriended Dr. Derrick Huang; a Harvard educated online marketing professor at Florida Atlantic University. Dr. Huang started to invite me into his classroom to teach a class on web analytics and online marketing. Of course, as you can see I do a lot more than web analytics so eventually, my discussions became a general discussion on the state of the web. One of the things I have learned about teaching is the more you teach, the more you become an expert on a subject. So whenever anyone asks me to teach, I usually fit it into my schedule. Typically this means I put my time in without getting paid. What I find is just the act of putting together class materials makes me research subjects and learn it well, before I teach it. While your time may be valuable, your time spent learning and becoming more of an expert is just as valuable.

After running the Startup Pitch Events for a year or so, we realized that startup founders were often not ready to pitch. Some had amazing products and services, but their pitch skill-sets were lacking. Let's just say many startups are started by engineers, programmers and financial experts and they have not worked on their communications and marketing skills.

A startup entrepreneur needs to be able to sell themselves

personally to an Investor. Investors invest as much as in the person than the idea.

It was obvious to me that we would need to train these tech startups. So we set up the first pitch training session on a weeknight, where 3 to 5 startup companies would come down to our space and spend a couple hours learning the art of pitching. We would have about 3 mentors as well. This to me was one of the ultimate mentoring sessions, where the startup would interact and listen to mentors. It would go back and forth where the startups would give their pitch and each mentor would then respond with comments, corrections, and recommendations.

Why did we do the mentoring?

Well, I found mentoring startups, just like teaching a class, we learn as much personally ourselves as the startups learned from the mentoring. But mentoring goes way beyond a few people standing around in a conference room going over their pitches.

The impact of mentoring was one of a dozen offline external activities that we did that had an impact on our personal authority in a subject matter. Mentoring gave me as many ideas for my blog articles as anything else I have ever done. While it may have appeared we were doing this for the startups, it was just as much of an exercise for ourselves, the mentors.

The mentoring sessions were listed on Meetup and Eventbrite and just that alone built up our authority on the subject matter. Every small piece of content that would appear on those Meetups and Eventbrite listings would get indexed and processed by Google.

Everything we cover in this book all leads you to get to be the authority on your subject matter and to be seen as a leader. To be viewed as a leader online is extremely is important for your personal SEO and will be the best way to be discovered by employers and found for work, but trust me it is hard to measure.

You have to just take a leap of faith when it comes to mentoring. My experience has been that those who give, get back 10 times more than what they put in.

So don't hesitate when that person you meet with asks for help with their career or their startup. Help them out! It will help you!

14

BE THE FUTURE

As a tech startup person and tech hack for the past 20 years watching the Internet change and grow, we always remember the tipping points, when a tech went from something tech guys played with to commercially viable and used by mass markets.

There have and always will be times when a technology seems like an unimportant footnote. There are tech winners and losers because not all tech gets accepted and used by the masses. A couple case in points is Archie, Lynx, Listserve, and Lisa if you know what these were.

There is a point where something hits the tipping point and you realize, "aha", this tech is changing things so much it will never be the same. One of those moments for me was when the first Instant Messenger app by AOL called AIM, was introduced. In the world of the Internet, AIM's introduction was one of the most important events for me personally. That's because it represented the very first time that people could interact via texting on our desktops instantaneously.   This was way before cell phone texting became a thing. Remember it is not how cool or when a tech was invented, it's important to understand when it will be used by millions for mass consumption! That's what we call *The Tipping Point.*

I was working at ABC distributing in North Miami on their website in 1999 when someone introduced me to AIM. I called my brother working in New York City and after he was set up with AIM we chatted live on our desktops. For both of us, it was a break-through, because we were not having a voice call and we were not reading emails. We were communicating live, real-time, by text. Obviously the next stages of technology and history of online chat is considerable.

What you have to start doing is reading and watching and recognizing when that new tech, apps, systems or tipping points happen, because the moment they happen with the Internet, there is always an opportunity.

For instance, in 1997 I noticed that Yahoo had introduced a new web service called Yahoo Store. Once again, pretty much not important today and no longer in business. What was important was that you could create an online store for free. It was another big break-through. I told my roommate from college about this and within months he was growing a very sizable online business with Yahoo.

This pattern of new tech and new opportunities has happened over 100 times in the past 20 years. Now we forget about the first time Facebook appeared or LinkedIn or Twitter or other social media. Each one of these new systems and tools allowed someone to master it and become an expert, even have their whole career revolve around that tech.

So, how do you recognize the future and not miss the boat? If you can sift through a lot of these new technologies that appear online and can figure out which ones are meaningful and which ones are not useful, you are going to have a major opportunity and it is also an opportunity to become a thought leader in the subject. I know a thought leader in the online dating industry very well who does very well, because of his expertise!

I am the first to say I have missed the boat on those 100 tech break-throughs, websites and apps that I could have been an expert at in the beginning. That's because tech people take a lot of tech for granted and are conservative by nature. I tend to wait around until others have tested the waters a bit. But as I started to run tech startup pitch events, I realized that the ability to decide and figure out which of these new techs would rule in the future and use them properly, and be one of the first users is a skill anybody can learn. You don't have to be young and you don't have to be smart. You do have to train yourself to know the difference between Uber and StumpleUpon. Nobody remembers StumpleUpon. And the power, money and early technology of the startup are not always the winner. Sometimes not so great tech sites control the future because they entered the right market at the right time, hence Meetup... Once a tech startup is successful at gaining critical mass, they can easily fix all the bugs later on.

So, why try to figure out *what's next*?

You need to be a master of what's new, what's hip, how it works and any new and different Internet systems in order to master your personal SEO and brand. It's all connected. Your ability to be intelligent and understand the world of the future in your industry can make or break your career. And all of this is pretty easy to do, if you just read a few online websites, some real print magazines, talk to your tech friends and keep your eyes wide open.

15

CONFERENCES & EVENTS AND SEO

Everybody eventually goes to industry events and conferences. While some industry events have gone online, the majority of conferences are still run in person. You need to understand the SEO value of these events for you personally by being involved as a speaker or panel member!

GO SEO YOURSELF TIP #15

PERSONAL MENTIONS ON CONFERENCE AND EVENT SITES ARE IMPORTANT SEO BACKLINKS AS WELL AS IMPORTANT LEADERSHIP INSIGNIAS

By being a speaker yearly at iDATE, the yearly online dating conference for industry professionals, I typically was listed on a website that had high authority on the subject matter. When employers see you provide thought leadership within an industry that elevates your profile!

There are tons of opportunities to be a speaker at local conferences, national conferences and to get up and be a leader at events. Many make a living as speakers. The online content generated by participating in these events is important for SEO and your career. Remember the event typically will list you on their website, often with a link back to your website. Imagine if you were a TEDx speaker. One major speaking engagement can change the level of authority you have in a specific market. Don't take this opportunity for granted.

Years after I was a speaker at events, I find links to my online listing, video and other content that spoke about. The impact on SEO using this technique is very strong.

16

OVERSEAS HEAD-HUNTERS

If you are in a desirable field and there is demand for your skills, there will be an ocean of headhunters looking for you. Overseas and outsourced headhunters currently dominate job lead generation. So you will have to deal with them! These are hired guns sitting in inexpensive places making calls for leads. It's a big business and they are very cost effective for their clients.

For me at least, I get 3 to 10 calls from outsourced head-hunters a day. One of the side effects of posting yourself and getting great SEO is that you will get found, and get found means tons of these third parties calling and emailing you, constantly.

Outsourced head-hunters always try to appear to be in the US with localized addresses and phone numbers on their emails. They will swear they are in a local city, but let's face it, they are not. They are part of a world of outsourcing, and until computers and AI robotics get good enough to replace them, they are here to stay.

I am not going to tell you that they are all bad. Some are nice people you can trust. But as you know they can be very annoying. They work on the premise that they will get a conversion per 500 calls. That means you are probably one of the 499 loss liters. That means they will very likely waste your time.

Occasionally they don't waste your time because they are typically connected to a real job somewhere. It just happens they sometimes get jobs that are great!

One time these outsourced headhunters ended up getting me an offer from Adobe Corporation, which I was grateful for, when it happened. I was offered a job through an Outsourced headhunter and third-party service to go and work as a contractor in San Jose for Adobe and I was actually given a start date and everything seemed to be working out.

It all depends on what you need today and how desperate you are. There are challenges like figuring out if outsourced head-hunters are ever worth using because they represent a major loss of personal value to a middleman.

The consulting job I landed that was arranged by outsourced head hunters with Adobe ended up not happening. I was told the Friday before I started that Adobe only wanted me 3 days a week as a consultant. Huh? I told them, a sure thing if I was a remote working, home-based in Florida. That situation turned into a no-go and by Monday it was over with Adobe.

Before my deal fell through I discovered I would be working for a subsidiary of the largest outsourced technology consulting firm in the world called TATA at 300,000 IT employees strong. That would have been acceptable. But actually, I would have been working for a small outfit named IDC based somewhere in India. There would be two consulting companies between me and Adobe.

I asked IDC who would be my boss, and the IDC guy said he would be my boss. That was really weird. Then I would be contracted out through the larger outsourced firm to Adobe. That means that the $70 an hour I was getting was more like $200 an hour, split between two Outsourced consulting firms both located overseas.

Let's just clarify something. I don't dislike outsourced head-hunters. They are doing what they are being paid to do. I actually like them. Though I sympathize with the plight of some of these head-hunters, this subcontractor job situation paying money out to a foreign entity to just get a job as a consultant in the US is nuts. So, I was not unhappy the deal fell through; though Adobe was at the top of my list for companies I desired to work for. I had to let it go from my mind! They had landed me in the doors of one of the companies I personally admired.

So, how to deal with the onslaught of outsourced headhunters?

It is pretty clear; let them all go to voicemail. Receive all the emails with the corrupt and invalid US mailing addresses. Let it all come in, but go through it carefully. Just like I was offered a gig at Adobe, there is sometimes a diamond in the rough, and that one time was really rough. I was saying in the year when I started my SEO job searching experiment I was contacted by no less than 500 outsourced recruiters. I could be off by 1,000. I have spent at least 1 minute reading their emails that would be 500 minutes. I have spent at least 5 minutes talking to 100 outsourced recruiters on the phone, answering their calls and having the same conversation every time. That is another 500 minutes. So, let's say it wasted 1,000 minutes or 15 hours of my life. So in the bigger picture, headhunters are not too bad of a distraction for a small possibility. It is better than the lottery. Just remember, let it go to voicemail. If you have the voice mail system which converts the voicemail to text, it is the way to weed through these headhunters.

The Dreaded References

After several bad experiences giving out references to head-hunters, I am now recommending not giving out references for a job opportunity until the employer has agreed to an interview. I have had head-hunters contact my references long before the employer agrees to a job interview and 9 out of 10 times I don't get the interview. Trust me; you don't want to wear out your references. You need to hold them as precious commodities because apparently, you can burn them out.

I have given specific instructions to head-hunters to not contact certain individuals and they have just ignored me. I have had the wrong reference on file. I wonder if that caused me to not get the interview. So, I plead with you to be very specific with a head-hunter to not contact references until you are further along in the process. In fact, I will drop the job request if they do not comply with my requirements. This is what I have learned. You have to be in charge of the situation, not the head-hunter. You control the rules and are not desperate for a job since another one will come along soon.

17

<u>MAKE SMART CHOICES WITH YOUR TIME</u>

One thing you need to consider when looking for a job is where to put your time. You need to value your time. You know what your hourly rates are! Even within this book, we will mention as many as 50 cloud-based systems you need to join, optimize. The work you need to put in to change your online career fortunes takes quite a bit of time.

How Do You Optimize Your Job Search Time

For some of us, this comes naturally. What happens to me is I have a number one priority job at any given time that I am working towards once the job hiring process starts. You have to look at your schedule and time and make sure you can both multi-task and prioritize.

For instance, I notice a lot of people attend job fairs. Technically speaking the odds of getting hired through a job fair is very similar to applying for a job online, though there is always a chance of making a connection with someone to be hired. To just leave your resume at a booth I have found to be a waste of time.

What you should have picked up from reading the top 10 resume sites you need to be on is that chapter is vitally important. And before the job far you needed to have already invested your time into creating your resume.

Instead of spending a day driving downtown to a job fair, you need to really consider the job things you need to be doing. And if you not on those 10 resume sites yet, it is time to start the work to add them.

A lot of people just start applying for every job possible on LinkedIn and through job listings on Indeed. My experience and I have quite a bit of experience, are those jobs once again being inundated with potentially hundreds if not thousands of resumes. If you are at my level of experience, you probably don't have an issue finding a job.

If you are just starting out in your career, spending time learning the process of building your resume, joining and creating your own community matter the most. You need to work not just your contacts, but pretty much everybody you have ever met. Most careers start by somebody reaching out and taking a chance on you.

Overall, you need to have goals that focus in on getting your online presence to a specific level. The first level would be at least to have a LinkedIn profile. The second level would be to make sure you have at least your resume on all 10 top job sites. The third level would be creating content; either blog or video related to the field you would like to work in. The next level is to create a community that can nurture your own career. This can be tough if you don't know what your career will be. Either way, you have to start somewhere.

18

<u>EMPLOYEE VS. CONSULTANT</u>

As you know many large employers will want to hire you as a consultant, at least for 6 months. Smaller and medium-sized employers tend to want to hire direct. Right off the bat, it would always seem that being an employee is the best option. At least this could be driven by the biggest issue of them all, healthcare. Now that I am back out on the market looking for another employer to take me on, I have to make sure our family is covered by health insurance. So, for me being a consultant seems to be a problem, and we don't have serious health issues in the family, but I can imagine if we did, we would probably be stuck!

I have been in both full-time and consulting roles over the years and most recently have gone back and forth between both states, and honestly, there are benefits to both.

But let's just look at the options and why we would consider one or the other. Do we have the choice between the option of being an employee and being a consultant? It is not always something we can control. But if you could control the choice between the two, let's look at the ups and downs.

Benefits of being a consultant:

Freedom to not have to be on the clock: Being a full-time 40 hour a week employee means you are typically locked in. A consultant does have some flexibility with timing, but there is also the fact that a consultant may have to work late into the night on projects.

Freedom in General: Seems like the moment I am working full-time for an employer, there is an immediate difference in how you are treated and what you can do is limited to the structure of the organization.

Ability to Negotiate Hourly Rate: At times in my career I wanted to be able to raise my rate as a consultant. You can negotiate your pay as a consultant, but once you are hired full-time, you have little to no negotiating ability for salary. You would need to wait until the end of the year or in some cases never.

Tax Benefits: As an independent consultant you typically have your own LLC or Corporation and you have the ability to take tax write-offs against the business. It seems like the new tax bill will be better for those with a corporation than those without one. Best to get your LLC ready for the next gig at least you will get the ability to write off expenses!

Benefits of being an employee

Less Unpredictability: Being an employee there should not be the unpredictability of consulting. I have had to fly out to remote cities as a consultant and meetings and projects can happen almost instantly. Full-time employee status means you know what is about to happen.

Benefits: Benefits are by far the main reason to be an employee. Unless you are building out a very large consulting firm with tons of employees who work for you or you can demand a very high hourly or project rate, then benefits can be as much as 30% of the value of working for a large employer.

Job Flexibility: I found while working as an employee I was able to flex and change and move into different job functions, especially at a large employer. At one employer working full time, I had 7 job titles and departments in 4 years. As a consultant, you typically are locked into a narrow scope job.

Management Skill: As a consultant, you rarely can be a manager, director or VP or CEO and very rarely will you be developed for management (if it still exists). Being a consultant means you will not be going to personal development training or management training. You will have to read articles like this one to get yourself trained!

I am sure there are a dozen reasons for one or the other. It is still clear to me that working as an employee is the better situation. Maybe it has more to do with where you are at in your career (if you are not starting up a business). If you are about to have kids and start a family, obviously being on a corporation's medical insurance is probably the biggest factor in why you would want to be an employee and not a consultant. If you had kids and they are long gone and you don't have a major medical problem, then consulting could be the way to go. Let me know what you think. I personally could be working as either in the next few months.

Either way tell me if you would rather work full-time, consultant, or run your own business (which could be just being a consultant!).

19

<u>DON'T RELY ON-LOOKERS</u>

One of the concepts I try to bring to a job search is the same concepts I learned in being an Ecommerce Director. When trying to drive traffic to a website through a marketing funnel, you have to differentiate the potential leads from those who are just looking at a product, surfing by and those that are serious about buying. The same thing is true about finding a job online.

Social media has proven for many small to medium-sized businesses to **not** be an effective method to market and convert sales for products. Social media, especially Facebook as well as Twitter, Pinterest and Instagram are considered by its users as a way to learn and entertainment and build email lists. It is a fool's errand to spend time and money on social media to drive most sales. Similar to TV advertising, social media is more of a branding medium than a selling medium. I am sure there are some examples of social media products out there, but I have yet to see any serious results. The results from marketing products on Facebook for instance typically have very low conversion rates if any, compared with email, texting, pay-per-click or organic searches. On the other hand conversions to events and for getting people to download free content on social media seem to be a different story.

That's because social networking sites like Facebook are not where people are looking to buy. They are online to just read and contribute. That's a group of people I call "Lookers".   Imagine having a store where people constantly came in and browsed but never purchased. You would be out of business right away. That's why you need to understand the difference between social media and other mediums that are more effective at converting like Amazon.com. Blogging, for instance, is a better medium for product conversion than social media because blogging allows you to fully explain what you are writing about and it gets great SEO if done properly. It is possible to blog and sell!

If you are looking for a job you can't waste your time on aspects of the web that are not important. Having your resume on job sites is critical to getting found. That's because it will continue to sell you through SEO long after you post your information. I have received calls where they mention a resume I put on the web 12 years ago. Being on LinkedIn and contributing articles and blog posts will get you found. Commenting on your friend's activities on Facebook will not get you found by employers!   If anything it will get you found for something you should not be doing!

So, if you are implementing your online SEO activities mentioned in this book for your job search, set priorities and make sure you don't go down paths that will not be fruitful.

I hope this book will have an impact on your job search, your career, and your life. If you really felt it had an impact please pass it along to a friend or family member! One comment I received while writing this book and discussing it with colleagues, other writers, friends and family is how many people said, "I need to send this book to someone I know". That was a good sign this book would be a great gift from a friend or family. That was my goal in writing this book; to have an impact on my colleagues, family and friends as well as yours!

Please feel free to email me anytime at dan@startuppop.com if you want to converse with me about any related subject. I would love to receive feedback about this book, areas that I did not cover properly or should have covered your thoughts or stories of how the book helped you. I would love to write these anecdotes into a second version with testimonies. Thank you for reading this book!

Dan Gudema

The List

This list of online cloud based services and tools are what you need to be focused on. I put this list together as a reminder of the tasks you need to accomplish in your job search:

Indeed.com
LinkedIn.com
Monster.com
Careerbuilder.com
Glassdoor.com
DICE.com
Job.com
SimplyHired.com
ZipRecruiter.com
Meetup.com
Eventbrite.com
HelpAReporter.com
Twitter.com
Facebook.com
Instagram.com
Pinterest.com
Youtube.com
Amazon.com
CreateSpace.com
GumRoad.com
PSCP.tv
ScreenCast-O-Matic.com
Medium.com
Fiverr.com
WordPress.com

Unsplash.com
Employerscorecard.com
Kindle.com
Uber.com

Dan Gudema

ABOUT THE AUTHOR

Though Dan Gudema aspired to be a writer as a kid, he was never able to fulfill his desire to be a published author till recently. Dan's goal has been to write a non-fiction book once a year and he has met that goal since 2014. Dan has worked as a corporate manager, programmer, entrepreneur and consultant. Dan is a fixture in the Start-Up community in South Florida and has worked for Bell Atlantic Mobile (now Verizon Wireless), ABC Distributing, NTT Corporation/Verio Inc., Office Depot and The Limited. In 2001 Dan co-founded and developed as a programmer Pre-Dating Speed Dating, which became the largest speed dating company in the US. Pre-Dating Speed Dating was sold to Cupid.com in 2004. Dan is the founder of StartupPOP, a Tech Startup Pitch Event which began in Boca Raton, FL. Originally from Parsippany, NJ, Dan moved to South Florida in 1997. Dan attended the University of Maryland for his BA and has an MBA from Florida Atlantic University.

Please visit Amazon.com for more books by Dan Gudema or email Dan with your thoughts at dan@startuppop.com or connect with Dan on twitter @dgudema or LinkedIn!